OXFORD WORLD'S CLASSICS

VIRGIL

T0025488

Georgics

Translated by
PETER FALLON

With an Introduction and Notes by
ELAINE FANTHAM

OXFORD
UNIVERSITY PRESS

OXFORD
UNIVERSITY PRESS

Great Clarendon Street, Oxford OX2 6DP

Oxford University Press is a department of the University of Oxford.
It furthers the University's objective of excellence in research, scholarship,
and education by publishing worldwide in

Oxford New York

Auckland Cape Town Dar es Salaam Hong Kong Karachi
Kuala Lumpur Madrid Melbourne Mexico City Nairobi
New Delhi Shanghai Taipei Toronto

With offices in

Argentina Austria Brazil Chile Czech Republic France Greece
Guatemala Hungary Italy Japan South Korea Poland Portugal
Singapore Switzerland Thailand Turkey Ukraine Vietnam

Oxford is a registered trade mark of Oxford University Press
in the UK and in certain other countries

Published in the United States
by Oxford University Press Inc., New York

First published as *The Georgics of Virgil* by Peter Fallon by The Gallery Press,
Loughcrew, Oldcastle, County Meath, Ireland in September 2004

This revised translation and Translator's Note © Peter Fallon 2004, 2006
Editorial material © Elaine Fantham 2006

British Library Cataloguing in Publication Data

Data available

Library of Congress Cataloging in Publication Data

Data available

ISBN 978–0–19–953883–6

15

Typeset in Ehrhardt
by RefineCatch Limited, Bungay, Suffolk
Printed in Great Britain by
Clays Ltd, Elcograf S.p.A.

for Adam

OXFORD WORLD'S CLASSICS

GEORGICS

PUBLIUS VERGILIUS MARO (VIRGIL) was born near Mantua in northern Italy in 70 BCE. He was educated at the larger town of Cremona and finally at Milan. He moved to Rome around 52 BCE, but spent most of his time thereafter in the (then) congenial surroundings of the Bay of Naples. He wrote the *Eclogues* in the period *circa* 42–39 BCE. Around the year 38 he joined the circle of poets in the entourage of Maecenas, the future imperial 'Minister for the Arts'. The composition of the *Georgics* occupied him from 37 or earlier until 29. He spent the rest of his life working on his epic poem, the *Aeneid*. He died at Brundisium in 19 BCE after abandoning a visit to Greece and Asia on which he intended to complete and perfect his epic.

PETER FALLON grew up on a farm near Kells in County Meath. He is a graduate of Trinity College, Dublin, where he was Writer Fellow in 1994. He was inaugural Heimbold Professor of Irish Studies at Villanova University in 2000. He founded The Gallery Press in 1970 and has edited and published more than 400 titles. His own books include *News of the World: Selected and New Poems* (1998). He lives in Loughcrew in County Meath.

ELAINE FANTHAM was educated at Oxford and taught first at the University of Toronto (1968–86) then Princeton University (1986–2000). She is author of commentaries on Seneca's *Trojan Women*, Lucan, *Civil War*, Book 2, and Ovid, *Fasti* IV, of *Roman Literary Culture*, and most recently of *Ovid's Metamorphoses* (Oxford Approaches to Literature) and *The Roman World of Cicero's De Oratore*.

OXFORD WORLD'S CLASSICS

*For over 100 years Oxford World's Classics have brought
readers closer to the world's great literature. Now with over 700
titles—from the 4,000-year-old myths of Mesopotamia to the
twentieth century's greatest novels—the series makes available
lesser-known as well as celebrated writing.*

*The pocket-sized hardbacks of the early years contained
introductions by Virginia Woolf, T. S. Eliot, Graham Greene,
and other literary figures which enriched the experience of reading.
Today the series is recognized for its fine scholarship and
reliability in texts that span world literature, drama and poetry,
religion, philosophy and politics. Each edition includes perceptive
commentary and essential background information to meet the
changing needs of readers.*

. . . cecini pascua rura duces
I sang of farms and fields and men who lead
Virgil, on his deathbed

CONTENTS

GEORGICS

INTRODUCTION

Virgil's Poem of the Land

Publius Vergilius Maro, the poet we know as Virgil, was born and spent his childhood in the fertile countryside of Andes, near the ancient Etruscan city of Mantua, 'by the waters | of the wide Mincius whose ambling course flows this way and that, | its sides tossing their fringe of wavy rushes.' (*Georgics* 3.13–15). We think of Mantua as Italian, but it and most of northern Italy had been inhabited by Gauls (Celtic tribes) until they were brought under Roman control by a series of campaigns ending about a century before Virgil's birth, on 15 October, 70 BCE. Geographically continuous with Roman territory, this region, roughly corresponding to Lombardy, was still treated in Virgil's youth as outside Italy proper, and governed as the province of Cisalpine Gaul. The elite acquired Roman citizenship through holding local magistracies, and were linked in family or friendship with Roman society, but the peoples of the Po basin would not become Roman citizens until their last governor, Julius Caesar, had the power to impose a law giving them citizenship when Virgil himself was in his twenty-first year, in 49 BCE.

Despite various reports by his biographers Virgil's father must have been a relatively prosperous farmer—or even landowner—and he was culturally ambitious, like the parents of Virgil's poetic predecessor Valerius Catullus from Verona, and of the contemporary historian Titus Livius (Livy) from Padua. He sent his son away to be educated, first for elementary instruction in language and literature at Cremona, then to Milan, and finally to prepare for public life by studying rhetoric at Rome itself.[1] But Virgil was not physically strong or socially confident, and his

---

[1] These details of Virgil's education come from Donatus' Life of Virgil (based on the biographer Suetonius), lines 21–5, in *Vitae Vergilianae*, ed. C. Hardie (Oxford, 1966). There is no English translation but a good discussion by Horsfall in *A Companion to Virgil* (Leiden, 1993).

father must have realized that his son was unsuited for the standard career of a lawyer or army officer. In fact both father and son may have taken active steps to avoid being involved in the civil war which broke out when Julius Caesar defied the Senate's attempts to control him and re-entered Italy with an army at Ariminum (near Mantua), in Virgil's twentieth year. The civil war divided the loyalties of many families, and most young Romans were caught up in the fighting between Caesar's forces and the forces of the senate commanded by Pompey, in northern Greece and later in North Africa and Spain.

Once the *Aeneid* made Virgil famous legends grew up around him, and a body of hexameter poems were ascribed to him; these, together with the poems and epigrams of the so-called *Catalepton* ('Miniatures'), were believed to be his youthful compositions.[2] Two epigrams are thought to be genuine and reflect the conflict between conventional education, his love of poetry, and his inclination to philosophy. One (*Catalepton* 5) puts rhetoric behind him, but cannot quite part with poetry:

Away! you hollow hype of the rhetoric teachers, words inflated with un-Greek froth, and you tribe of pedants . . . dripping with unguent; away! you hollow cymbals of youth, and farewell to you, preoccupation of my affections, Sextus Sabinus, farewell my fine fellows. We are setting sail for the blessed harbours, in search of the wise words of great Siro, and we have freed our life of all preoccupation.

Away! Muses, you too, go now, sweet Muses (for I admit the truth— you have been sweet to me), and yet come back to visit my notebooks, but seldom and with restraint.

Siro was the respected Epicurean teacher who lived in private simplicity at Naples, the city given autonomy by Rome out of respect for its Greek origin and culture. We do not know how long Virgil stayed with Siro, but he writes in the coda to the *Georgics* (about twenty years later) that he is 'lying in the lap of Naples, quite at home | in studies of the arts of peace' (*Georgics*

[2] This is the so-called *Appendix Vergiliana* (ed. W. V. Clausen, Oxford, 1966); I know of no English translation, so have offered my own version of the epigrams.

4.563–4). Another short poem (*Catalepton* 8) seems to look back with loving memory on Siro and his little world:

Little house that belonged to Siro, and poor little plot, real riches for him as master, I commend myself to you and along with me the friends I have always loved and foremost my father, should I hear any grim news of my country. You will now be for him what Mantua had been, and Cremona earlier still.

It is difficult to rid ourselves of hindsight and preconceptions, but we should realize that the young Virgil had no reason in 40 BCE to imagine he would compose anything like the *Georgics*, an unprecedented poem, or his great epic. He had clearly read and loved Lucretius and Catullus, and poets like Catullus' friend Calvus and the love-elegist Cornelius Gallus, whose work is now virtually lost to us. But what he did compose, some time between 40 and 35 BCE, were his *Bucolics* or *Eclogues*, a set of ten hexameter poems, apparently simple shepherd songs modelled on the pastoral poems of Theocritus, a sophisticated third-century poet from Cos who wrote for the courts of Syracuse and Alexandria.

Virgil's *Eclogues* vary from skilful imitations of the song contests imagined by Theocritus, to the ecstatic prophecy of the new golden age (*Eclogue* 4) that would begin with a marvellous child, and tributes to the mythical and erotic poetry of his predecessor Gallus (*Eclogues* 6 and 10): most are apparently set in Sicily or in Arcadia, the hilly and remote land of the Peloponnese. But two poems, the first and the ninth, are set in Virgil's homeland and reflect some of the hardships its people suffered from renewed civil war after Caesar's death. Several cities in Virgil's region, notably Cremona, were obliged to Mark Antony as patron and had joined his supporters against Octavian. When Octavian emerged as victor he penalized them by confiscating their land to provide homes and farms for his veteran soldiers, and it seems that Virgil's family property was treated as the territory of Cremona and would have been forfeit if Asinius Pollio, the historian and destined consul of 40 BCE had not intervened to restore it.[3]

---

[3] Cf. *Georgics* 2.198–9: 'rolling plains such as Mantua was misfortunate enough to lose, | where graceful swans are flourishing in weedy waters.'

Little as we know about what happened, these two *Eclogues* reflect the uneven fortunes of local farmers. In the first poem Meliboeus contrasts Tityrus' fortune to be resting in his own shade when Meliboeus himself must leave 'the boundaries and sweet ploughlands of home'.[4] There is disruption all over the countryside, and he fancies that he will have to go to alien lands like Africa or Syria. In contrast, Tityrus explains that he went to Rome where a divine young leader gave him both his freedom (he has been a slave until now) and his land. It is not good land, mere pasture covered with stones and choked with marsh, but it is cool with springs and alive with birds and bees.

Tityrus treats the young leader as a god and will offer him monthly sacrifice. This is Virgil's tribute to Octavian, whether or not it reflects his own experience.[5] The ninth *Eclogue* is more melancholy. Moeris is going to town with a gift for the new owner of his land, and tells Lycidas how the stranger came and evicted him with the crude words, 'this property is mine: old tenants, out!' It seems that Moeris was farming as a tenant, and with the change of ownership has been expelled. Lycidas had heard that Menalcas (usually considered to be Virgil himself) had saved all this stretch of land 'from where the hills | begin to drop down, sloping gently from the ridge, | right to the water and the old beeches' broken crown', by his songs. If we read this poem literally then Virgil's appeal to power has been in vain, at least for Moeris. The two shepherds travel together for the first part of their way recalling Menalcas' songs (snatches of verse from *Eclogues* 2, 3, and 5) and looking forward to Menalcas' return.

Did Virgil return? It is likely that his property survived, if only because he came early to the notice of Octavian's friends, both Asinius Pollio, administering his land grants in the region, and

---

[4] This and all subsequent quotations from *Eclogues* are from the translation of Guy Lee (1980).

[5] P. Veyne, 'L'Histoire agraire et la biographie de Virgile dans les Bucoliques I et IX', *Revue de Philologie* (1980), 233–57, uses the poems to reconstruct where Virgil's father had his farm and to interpret Tityrus as a slave entrusted by his master Octavian with a plot of land from which to earn his freedom. But Tityrus is the product of a poet's imagination, and Veyne is more valuable as commentator on agrarian conditions than for any factual light on the poet.

Cilnius Maecenas, who used his wealth to sustain poets such as Virgil, Horace, Propertius. Virgil's biographers claim he spent three years composing the *Eclogues*, and seven on his next, more ambitious poem, the *Georgics*, whose four books he read to Octavian over four successive days on Octavian's return from Actium and Alexandria in 29 BCE.[6] Donatus also offers a glimpse of how he worked, composing a number of verses in the early morning, then spending the day refining and reducing them to a very few, licking them into shape—so he said—like a mother bear her cubs. Seven years would place the beginning of Virgil's new poem in 36 BCE, in harmony with the evidence for his friendship with Maecenas and the appearance in 37 of a very important prose work on Italian farming, the 80-year-old Varro's *De re rustica*. Varro's three books, the first on arable farming, the second on pasturing cows, horses, sheep, and pigs, and the third on *villatica pastio*, small-scale garden operations like beekeeping, provided a potential framework for Virgil's art.[7]

The title *Georgics* probably needs more than one English equivalent to convey its meaning, because it relates both to the Greek phrase for 'working the land' and to the noun *geourgos*, or 'farmer': we could call it 'the farmer's life', but Virgil's stress is as much on the continuing relationship between the worker and the earth as it is on his daily or yearly work. Virgil's poems too are very difficult to describe or analyse, for several reasons: part agricultural manual, with instructions to the farmer on dealing with crops, vines, and olives, livestock, and (surprisingly) bees, they are also in part political poem and allegory. Although they are usually classified in the Greek and Latin tradition of didactic verse, they are an entirely new kind of poem. The four books are balanced against each other in a complex structure that can be characterized in many ways; the world evoked by the poem is caught up in a critical moment for Rome and Italy as the chaos of civil war is

---

[6] Donatus, Life, lines 91–7. The following quotation is from lines 81–4.

[7] On Virgil's use of Varro in the *Georgics*, see R. F. Thomas, *Reading Virgil and his Texts: Studies in Intertextuality* (Ann Arbor, 2000), chs. 5 and 8.

becoming a benevolent but unacknowledged monarchy; and we as readers risk blinding ourselves to what Virgil is (and is not) saying with our previous sentimental attachments to the countryside or to Italy itself.

It is perhaps best to start with the tradition of 'didactic poetry'.[8] This is not a genre recognized by ancient critics even a century after Virgil's death, but it has become a useful critical category. One obvious division is between poetry that teaches how to exercise an art, and poetry that sets out a body of knowledge—such as the map of the stars (Aratus before Virgil, Manilius after him) or at its most ambitious the nature of the material world described by the Epicurean Lucretius in his great poem in six books *On the Nature of the Universe*. This poem sets out the atomic structure of the physical world, of our psychological world, and of climatic and cosmic phenomena. If Virgil revered his Epicurean teacher Siro, he still rejected Epicurean beliefs about divine indifference, and passionately advocated devout worship of the gods. But the powerful language of Lucretius' poetry had a greater influence on Virgil's language in the *Georgics* than any other Latin poet. The other kind of didactic, that gave instruction in an art or sport, looks like a model for Virgil to instruct the farmer, but normally took a far more trivial form, providing exercise for the many educated amateurs to compose works on hunting or dicing, and a conventional framework for Virgil's most talented successor, Ovid, to create his parodic *Art of Love*.

As recent scholarship has shown, Virgil has applied in his *Georgics* not only the learning of Greek and Roman prose treatises but a wealth of poetic memories from Homer, whose heroic narrative poems were also seen by the ancient world as a source of teaching, from Hesiod's two great poems, *Works and Days* and *Theogony* with their precepts for good farming and virtuous living in relation to men and gods, and from a range

---

[8] A. Dalzell, *The Criticism of Didactic Poetry: Essays on Lucretius, Virgil and Ovid* (Toronto, 1998) is a wise and accessible study (ch. 4 on *Georgics*) that should be better known outside Canada: see also K. Volk, *The Poetics of Latin Didactic: Lucretius, Vergil, Ovid, Manilius* (Oxford, 2002), ch. 4.

of Alexandrian poets.[9] Besides Aratus, whose weather lore Virgil adapts extensively in Book 1 of the *Georgics*, Virgil adapts Eratosthenes' account of the five zones of the globe, Nicander's poem on serpent venom and its cures (*Theriaca*) and surely at least in part Nicander's *Georgica*.[10] It is also important to take into account the aetiologies and narrated myths of Callimachus' *Aitia*, his composite collection of elegies in four books, which have more subtle equivalents in the framing of Virgil's own four books. Virgil does not plaster allusions onto the continuous thought of his poetry but incorporates echoes and reminiscences for his poetry-loving readers to enjoy.

One defining aspect of 'didactic' is its non-narrative, descriptive or prescriptive content: another is its addressee. But no poem has more levels of addressee than the *Georgics*. An addressee may be pupil or patron, as Memmius, however unsatisfactory, was pupil and patron of Lucretius. But Virgil's patron Maecenas is not his pupil. In each book Virgil addresses Maecenas, with a simple apostrophe in the second line of his text in Books 1 and 4 and with a more detailed account of his intention in Books 2 (lines 39–46) and 3 (lines 40–5), where he describes his enterprise as ordered by Maecenas ('no little task that you've laid out for me, Maecenas'). But once addressed, Maecenas plays no part in the main body of each book. Virgil's pupils are supposedly the farmers whom he often addresses, but it is difficult to identify what kind of farmer Virgil had in mind. In any case it is unlikely that his reader would consider making his own plough from found timber (1.169–75). Virgil offers instructions as an allusive tribute to Hesiod, who had done so in the earliest Greek poem on farming, his *Works and Days*. Well-off Romans all owned land, or

---

[9] The chief scholarly discussions of Virgil's art of allusion are Thomas, in his two-volume commentary (Cambridge, 1988) and essay collection (1999, above n. 7) and J. Farrell, *Virgil's Georgics and the Tradition of Ancient Epic: The Art of Allusion in Literary History* (Oxford, 1991).

[10] Thomas (1999), 137–40, has identified allusions to seven Greek and Latin poets in Virgil's adaptation of this passage alone. Virgil adapts Nicander's *Theriaca* for his account of antidotes to snakebite in *Georgics* 3.414–39, and probably for his vivid botanical description of the curative flower *amellus* (4.271–80): too little survives of Nicander's *Georgica* to establish a link between them.

aimed to do so, and had it farmed by slaves under the supervision
of a bailiff; they valued the land as a superior source of produce
for their own use, but also for the market. Less-well-off Romans
and Italians usually made intensive use of the little land they
possessed, and Virgil provides a delightful, if fantastic, example
of such a humble gardener in his account of the old man of
Tarentum (4.125–48).[11] But in his poem he exploits a Roman
linguistic feature, which credited a man with doing whatever
he had done for him by subordinates, to instruct the farmer
directly.[12] He may use impersonal phrases of obligation, or
describe the farmer's task and methods, or use the second person
either in straight imperatives or advisory future tenses, but he will
not mention slaves: there is only the occasional generic reference
to countrymen or tenants. As Seneca said (*Epistulae Morales*
86.16), Virgil was essentially composing his poem not to instruct
actual farmers but to give pleasure to his readers. (It is not within
the scope of this introduction to discuss Italian crops or farming
methods: some useful works are listed in the Select Bibliography.)

I have postponed one unprecedented addressee, the one
who usually causes most alienation in modern readers, Caesar
(Octavianus), the future Augustus, who is not simply addressed
but invoked as a god-in-the-making for half of Virgil's great
divine invocation opening Book 1. Unlike Rome's first agri-
cultural writer, M Porcius Cato, writing more than a century
earlier, Varro had given his *De re rustica* a religious setting—at the
festival called Sementiva (Sowing) in the temple of Tellus—and
an invocation to twelve gods who sustain all the produce of the
fields on earth and in the sky: Jupiter and Tellus (Earth), the
great parents, Sun and Moon as markers of the seasons, Ceres
and Liber (Bacchus), Robigo and Flora, the negative and positive
powers controlling the fruiting of blossom, Minerva and Venus,
goddesses of the olive and the vegetable garden, Lympha, the

---

[11] On this passage, see Thomas (1999), ch. 6, 'The Old Man Revisited'.

[12] J. M. Frayn, *Subsistence Farming in Rome and Italy* (London, 1979) notes that most
Roman agricultural writers seem to vary between addressing the landowner and the
smallholder or tenant farmer, but that this creates no problem, since the same methods
would be used in large- or small-scale farming.

spirit of running water and Bonus Eventus (Happy Outcome). Virgil, too, follows his brief enumeration of contents with a multiple invocation, to twelve gods or groups of gods: Sun and Moon ('grand marshals of the firmament'), Liber and Ceres, then the country demigods, 'Fauns, and maiden Dryads', Neptune as patron of horses, and a hero new to Latin cult, Aristaeus, 'patron of shady woods', Greek Pan, 'caretaker of the flocks', Minerva as patroness of the olive, Greek Triptolemos, 'that youth . . . creator of the crooked plough', and Sylvanus, all gods 'whose care and concern is | for land' (lines 21–2). It is at this point that he turns to Octavian.

While the traditional gods have been addressed because they protect the farmer's world, Virgil assumes that Octavian too will become a god, and the only issue is whether he will choose to be god of earth or sea or sky (given apotheosis as a constellation). He appeals to the young leader both for his poem and for the farmers: 'grant me an easy course, and bless the boldness of this undertaking— | who shares my sympathy for countrymen whose lives are wanderings in the dark' (lines 40–1). Virgil asks Octavian to join him in taking pity on the inexperienced farmers and accept their vows and prayers.

Poets had traditionally invoked the Muses or Apollo to inspire their work; now for the first time a poet appeals to a mortal—and subsequent poets would feel bound to pay homage in this way to princes and emperors. The political power of Octavian is paramount and the extreme hardships of civil war explain the real urgency of the poet's treatment. Octavian is not addressed again in the *Georgics* but he is kept prominent. At the end of Book 1, as Virgil recalls the sun showing pity for Rome at Julius Caesar's death and the portents reflecting divine distress and anger, he turns to 'Romulus, god of our fathers, strength of our homes, our mother Vesta', begging the gods not to begrudge Octavian to men on earth, but spare him to quell wars that have robbed the fields of farmers, vicious civil wars and foreign uprisings over the entire earth. In the closing image the young charioteer who must fight his team for control of the reins is Octavian himself.

Octavian is only glimpsed in Book 2, warding off the remote

and unwarlike Indians from the Capitol (2.170–2)[13]—but is central to the extraordinary and grandiose proem to Book 3. In this Hellenistic tour de force, Virgil echoes the celebratory odes composed for victorious athletes by Pindar, and Callimachus' poem honouring the chariot victory of his Alexandrian patron Queen Berenice which similarly opens the third book of his *Aitia*.[14] But first Virgil rejects the old mythological subjects focusing on Hercules and Pelops (who won a bride and a kingdom by cheating in a chariot race), and proclaims his desire to win lasting poetic fame[15] and bring 'the prize of the Muses' back to Mantua (3.3–15). He will erect a temple to Caesar (Octavian) and make him the centre of the poetic celebration. As Octavian himself erected a temple for his deified adoptive father Julius, so Virgil will create—or is now creating—a poetic temple, honouring the victories over Antony and Cleopatra at Actium and Alexandria as Octavian did, with a monument (and a city, Nicopolis) and annual victory games. Assimilating himself to both the victor in the four-horse chariot race (line 18) and the Roman magistrate who presided (line 21) over the sacrifice at festivals and the celebratory games and races, Virgil plans to make his beloved Mincius the envy and destination of all Greece. To the races (appropriate to his treatment of horse-breeding) he adds a theatre, such as Roman magistrates often constructed for temporary performances, with conquered barbarian peoples (and not yet conquered, such as Britain, Parthia, and India) on the stage curtains and temple doors, and he adorns the scene with precious statues of (Caesar's) Trojan ancestors, while jealousy and sin are trampled underfoot like enemy captives (lines 24–39).

[13] This cannot pass without comment. What glory is there in warding off unwarlike or 'craven' enemies? The Indians were not involved in any fighting at this time, and remained utterly remote from the Capitol. Irony is out of the question in this context, but the line may allude to diplomatic approaches from India (cf. Augustus' own record, *Res Gestae* 31), seen as a reflection of their fear of Octavian. We know of appeals from later Indian rulers in 25 and 20 BCE.

[14] See Thomas (1999), ch. 2, especially pp. 89–90, and Conte, 'Proems in the Middle', *Yale Classical Studies*, 29 (1992), 147–59.

[15] The phrase 'live on in the mouths of men' (3.9) quotes a famous line of his epic predecessor Ennius, who also celebrated a military hero, Scipio Africanus.

Scholars are divided on whether Virgil is already anticipating his next great poem, which will become the *Aeneid*, or enacting the imperial praise by these verses. It is difficult for modern readers to accept this pomp, particularly in the simpler context of the Italian farm, but this is the book in which Virgil will celebrate thoroughbred warhorses and sacrificial bulls (already honoured in 2.145–8); a brief allusion to pasturage (represented as Dryads' woods) and to Maecenas' commands is matched with a promise which seems to commit the poet more explicitly to a patriotic epic: 'That time's not far away when I'll have girt myself to sing of Caesar's hard-fought battles | and guarantee he'll live, in name and fame, down all the years' (3.46–7). And Octavian will return at the end of Book 4, the close of the work, depicted in a thundering attack on the rebellious Euphrates, 'adding victory to triumph, winning the war for people who appreciate his deeds, | and laying down the law—enough to earn his place in heaven' (4.561–2).[16] Military triumph is the prerequisite of legitimate empire and the ruler's role as lawgiver and just judge that Hesiod too saw as the mark of kings cherished by the gods. What is new is the expectation of actual divinity.

I have lingered over these elements in the hope of making them less strange to readers who approach this poem with a romantic yearning for rural simplicity. Within its courtly frame the *Georgics* soon gets down to earth, but involves the reader in a constantly changing play of emotions. Structurally, Virgil's four books permit a number of patterns: the gradual increase of partnership between farmer and produce, from anonymous grain and pulse to more individualized vines and trees (protected like children from harsh conditions, 2.265–72), to the ardent ambitions of racehorses in training, the sexual passions of the animal world, and the pathos of helpless small cattle, and finally the complex community of selfless and sexless bees who are assigned to different services (4.149–69) and often 'pay the final

---

[16] Here and elsewhere the Euphrates stands for Rome's enemy, Parthia, which had twice inflicted defeat in previous years. Augustus would achieve a face-saving settlement through diplomacy in 20–19 BCE.

sacrifice— | such is their love for flowers and pride in the production of the honey' (4.204–5).

Scholars have also stressed the alternation between 'pessimism' and 'optimism' as the reiterated stress on work in Book 1 ('Hard work prevailed, hard work and pressing poverty' 1.146, in Virgil a present statement of the harsh law of nature) gives way to the passages in Book 2 singing praise of Italy, of spring, and of the old-fashioned country life. In the same way Book 3 foreshadows early, with the much-quoted 'Poor creatures that we are, the best days of our lives | are first to fly' (3.66–7), the progressively more distressing accounts, first of desperate animal (and human) passion, then of sickness and death polluting the countryside, aborting sacrifice, and reducing men to draught animals dragging their own carts and ploughs (3.536). But the sickness that destroys Aristaeus' bees in Book 4 is remedied by his obedient and faithful performance of ritual instructions so that this last book ends in a kind of resurrection.

Another 'structural' feature is surely the tension between the end of Book 2, seen as closure of the pair of books presided over by Ceres and Liber (1.7–9, cf. Ceres 1.96, 147, 163, 338–50, and Bacchus/Liber, 2.2–8, 229, 380–96, 454–7, 529) and the continuity it invites with Book 3 through its evocation of Rome's golden past juxtaposed with hopes of present and future glory.

Book One

Given the vivid physical world and the multi-layered poetic inheritance of these books, a short introduction[17] can only sample some aspects of each book, just as Virgil himself chose only to sample from the instructions which a farmer would require. In considering each book it will be helpful to bear in mind the contrast between the topics Virgil has chosen and what was available to him, especially in Varro's three books. Varro's work is both pragmatic and antiquarian in his enjoyment of religious and

---

[17] See the introduction to Thomas's commentary (1988), vol. i. R. A. B. Mynors' fine commentary (*Virgil: Georgics* (Oxford 1990)) was published posthumously and so has no introduction.

cultural history. Thus his first book, covering arable farming, vineyards, olive groves, and orchards, shares with Virgil comments on the origin of the animal sacrifices to Ceres and Liber—but while Virgil explains the offering of goats to Liber by their offence in nibbling at young vine stems, he suppresses the offence of pigs sacrificed to Ceres, as he does all discussion of swine, the staple animal of Italian peasant holdings.[18] Varro's second book, like Virgil's third, focuses on pasturing, but dilates on the antiquity of the pastoral life: it gives pigs (2.4) as much attention as horses (2.7) and in dealing with each animal pays attention to the forms and requirements of sale. And finally the bees which fill Virgil's last book occupy only one long chapter (3.16) of Varro's more miscellaneous study of new and exotic foods that can be raised in the gardens and yards around the country house.

In fact the grain crop itself takes up only a small fraction of Book 1 of the *Georgics*, in which Virgil is preoccupied with the elements: soil and landscape, water and sky, both the predictable seasons of the year and unpredictable weather. He begins with spring ploughing, but turns first to soil quality and choosing the right crop for one's soil and site, to preparing the land with rake and mattock and supplying it with irrigation and fighting various pests. Well before he adapts his description of how to make a plough from Hesiod's *Works and Days*, Virgil introduces what is often called a theodicy, a myth to justify the incessant and arduous work of the farm, in a reinterpretation of Hesiod's five races of men, sinking from the happy leisure of the golden race to the vicious warfare of the present age of iron. Before men devised the concept of property, they shared in common the lavish and spontaneous produce of the earth. It was Jupiter who made their lives difficult by creating pests and suppressing wine and honey and natural fire, not to punish men for wickedness as in Hesiod, but to challenge them to work and devise necessary crafts, making boats and steering them by the stars, hunting, fishing, and carpentry, and it was Ceres who taught agriculture when acorns

---

[18] See Varro, *De re rustica* 1.2.19 on goat sacrifice to Bacchus; 2.4.9 on sacrificing pigs to Ceres. The animal sacrifice to Ceres at *Georgics* 1.345 goes unidentified but should be a piglet. Swine are mentioned in passing at 1.400, 2.520, and 3.497.

and berries proved too scanty a source of food. This hardship was for man's own good. Virgil's god (or gods) is providential, and it is by divine providence that two of the universe's five climatic zones are tempered ('a pair of zones is given | by godly grace to pitiful man') between the icy poles and torrid equatorial region (1.231–51). Here Virgil colours the original Hellenistic description of Eratosthenes, in reaction against Lucretius' pessimistic portrait of an earth made increasingly unfit for man by adverse climate, terrain, and failing fertility.[19] The regularity of the year is a gift of the sun, just as the second part of this book pays tribute to the benevolent signs given by the sun to man of both natural weather and human offences against the gods.

This first book also instructs the farmer in his calendar, using the stars as his guide (cf.1.1–2, 'by what star | to steer the plough'). Varro had divided the year into eight half-seasons, defined by the winter and summer solstices and the equinoxes, the Favonius or west wind of spring, the rising and setting of the Pleiades, and the scorching season of the Dog Star. Virgil gives a sample, evoking in one verse that fuses half-lines of Homer and Callimachus, 'the Pleiades, the Hyades, and Lycaon's child, the glittering Great Bear' (1.138), and warning (1.335–7) about the need to watch each month's constellations, and the planets of Saturn and Mercury. Early Greek poets had other ways of marking the calendar, and Virgil offers a sample of Hesiod's lucky and unlucky days of the moon at 1.276–86, but he does not forget the farmer's own experiences at different times of day and year— his work after dark in winter as his wife weaves beside him, the gathering of berries and hunting of small game in winter, the tragic wind storms that ruin the crops before harvest, and the rain storms that flood the fields. Rain is in fact the link to his next theme—the non-seasonal weather signs treated by the Hellenistic poet Aratus. Aratus had followed his description of the sky with weather signs drawn from sun and moon and animal behaviour. Virgil reverses the order, because he will bring the book to a climax in the eclipse of the sun in grief over Julius Caesar's death:

[19] Cf. Lucretius 5.783–836, esp. 826–36.

so he gives us first the response to coming rain of heifers, swallows, frogs, and ants, of many kinds of birds, seagulls, rooks, and crows in vivid vignettes; to Aratus' physical details he adds here a denial that the birds were divinely inspired, in favour of a materialist explanation as a physical reaction to change in what we would call barometric pressure (1.374–429). (He will more willingly embrace the divine inspiration of bees in Book 4.)

Moon signs and sun signs are enriched with mythical allusions, as Virgil leads to the many portents that function both as grief for Caesar's murder and warning of the ensuing civil conflicts. There is a terrible power in the cumulative list of natural disasters world wide (Etna, Germany, the Alps, the Po, and the Thracian battlefield of Philippi), as some future farmer turns up rusty weapons and human bones in his fields which have been robbed of their cultivation by the endless sequence of war (1.471–97). While Virgil often compares the farmer's struggle with recalcitrant woodland and fields to warfare, this book finds its poignancy in the opposition of farming and killing. Only if the young driver Octavian can control his chariot will peace in the remote empire and between neighbouring (Italian) cities be restored.

Book Two

The second book is almost exultant with the lavish variety of the land and the exuberant growth of its fruits. It is not surprising that scholars such as Ross and Thomas have protested at Virgil's eagerness to boast of incredible grafts and credit Italy with equal productivity of soil and manpower.[20] There is an excitement which will return in Book 3 (284–93), as Virgil enhances his theme of variety by a parade of exotic products from remote Arabia and India and Ethiopia, but none of these lands can match 'this land of ours' (2.140). Varro had begun his study by praising Italy for the abundance and superiority of its products. Virgil maintains this spirit, celebrating Italy's olives and vines, oxen and

[20] D. Ross, *Virgil's Elements: Physics and Poetry in the Georgics* (Princeton, 1987), 104–9; Thomas (1999), 156–8, 170–2.

horses, with 'constant spring—and summer out of season' (line 149) that bring forth double harvests, but also for the achievements of its peoples, cities and towns on mountaintops, rivers and great lakes as well as engineering feats like the 'Julian harbour' (created by Agrippa to provide inland naval docks in Campania) and rich mines of silver and gold. The poet actually gives more space to Italy's manpower and Rome's leaders, culminating in Caesar, than to her natural glories, saluting the land as 'holy mother of all that grows, | mother of men' (lines 173–4).

A survey of different types of land and their varying suitability to different types of farming looks forward to pasture (lines 195–202), back to good ground for grain crops, some brutally cleared of undisturbed woodland 'the ancient habitats of birds' (line 209), and to dry soil, barely fit for bees, while thirsty land exhaling mist and rich in grass is good for every kind of farming: prolific in vine-laden elms and in olives, friendly to cattle and responsive to the plough. The farmer needs detailed instruction on how, where, and when to plant his seedlings before the poet refreshes him with a hymn to spring, the season when the marriage of father sky and mother earth nourishes every kind of shoot, season of birdsong and animal desire (line 329 looks forward to Book 3). There must have been the same abundance of thrusting growth at the world's first creation, when the great globe enjoyed spring and the first cattle and human offspring of earth raised their heads, when beasts were sent to populate the woods, and stars in the sky (lines 336–45). I am paraphrasing to bring out how here, and again towards the end of this book, Virgil leaps back to the beginning of history and associates present country life with an imagined golden past. Virgil's description of the Bacchic festival, the origin of drama, will find a counterpart in the athletic contests he mentions as the book nears its close: but first he gives brief attention to undemanding olives, to orchard fruits and all the useful trees, rushes, and reeds that provide wattle and fencing for the farm.

After a disturbing afterthought on the harm that can be done by men drunk with abuse of Bacchus' gifts, Virgil leaves them for a long coda on the blessings of country life, beginning with what ancient rhetoricians called a *makarismos*: 'They're steeped in luck, country people . . . earth that's just | showers them with all that they could ever ask for' (lines 458–60). Here and elsewhere he delights in a wishful thinking that ignores the hardships he himself has spelled out. We know this is no easy living. Why does Virgil encourage such expectations? I believe the explanation lies in the ancient love of paradoxography, the fantasy literature of marvels. This 'quiet life—carefree and no deceit— | and wealth untold' (lines 467–8) is a fairy tale such as we all believe when we first plant our gardens or move to a new home—and it quickly gives way to the more realistic 'young men wed to meagre fare but born and built for work', but not without Aratus' myth of the maiden Justice who lingered last among these peasants when she abandoned the earth.[21]

Does Virgil see himself as one of them? He begs the Muses whose art he loves to welcome him and explain the ways of the natural world (lines 475–82), but if he falters, to let him delight in the country, and live without glory, loving rivers and woods in romantic Greek wilderness. A second *makarismos* offers another choice of stronger and weaker achievement, contrasting the man who was able to discover the causes of nature and trample fear of death and Acheron under his feet (lines 490–2), with another who only knows the country gods, Pan and old Sylvanus. There is a deliberate blurring here between the life lived and the poetry written, but just as lines 490–2 come so close to naming Lucretius, the poet of the natural world, that we read the man who knows the country gods as another kind of poet, so the earlier choice should probably be taken as a choice of poetic theme rather than between two kinds of life, one of scientific study and one of shepherding. Countryman or country poet: both escape political ambition and the greed that drives men to restless travel, to mercenary warfare and the life of the court, to fratricide and exile. Like Lucretius, Virgil rejects outright the values of the Roman elite.

---

[21] Aratus, *Phaenomena* 96–136.

When Virgil returns for the last time to the farmer he acknow-
ledges the heavy work of ploughing, but ties the unresting toil of
the farmer's year to the abundance he must gather in even in
winter. In a final vignette he presents the countryman pouring
libations to Bacchus at his festival (line 529; cf. line 388),
presiding over a little world of virtuous family, cattle, and young
goats, as his shepherds compete in javelin throwing and wrestling.
We have seen that this may be a less glorious life than that of
the philosophical poet, and more strenuous, but far happier than
the way urban Romans seek their glory. Now just as Virgil saw the
beauty of each spring as like the primeval spring of creation, so
he sees the happiness of country relaxation as the life once lived
by Romulus and the Etruscan neighbours who made Rome great.
It is the original good life of Saturn (first evoked in 1.121–8),
before Jupiter became king and men learnt to feast on their own
plough-oxen and make themselves weapons and answer the call
to battle. The poet has taken his readers far in space and further
in time; no wonder he speaks of unyoking his horses after this
immense poetic journey.

Book Three

The third book begins, as we saw, with the fanfare of Virgil's
proposed poetic temple to Augustus, but this should not obscure
its simple invocation to Pales, the patron deity of herds and
flocks. Two invocations to Pales divide the book into the treat-
ment of breeding large animals (lines 1–283) and small (lines
295–566), but the first section also invokes Apollo, who once
served as a herdsman, and whose Olympian associations are bet-
ter suited to the heroic themes of breeding thoroughbred horses
and sacrificial cattle. Again, Virgil is selective, treating only the
ideal female cow and male horse, the training of colts (whose
natural ardour for racing he evokes in lines that will return to
describe the Trojan oarsmen in Aeneas' boat-race), the protection
of pregnant cows and mares, and the battles of bulls for suprem-
acy. In keeping with his words in *Eclogues* 3.101, 'alike to herd and
herdsman love is ruinous', he builds the climax of this section out

of the universal passion: 'Man and beast, each and every race of earth, | creatures of the sea, domesticated animals, and birds in all their finery, | all of them rush headlong into its raging fury' (lines 242–4): at its heart Leander's desperate crossing of the Hellespont to visit his beloved Hero (lines 258–63) is matched by the unbridled ferocity of mares (lines 264–83) until Virgil realizes he has been carried away by his theme and turns to vulnerable sheep and goats.

Virgil's gentle precepts for pasturing sheep in Italy's mild climate are offset by ethnological portraits of shepherding in the extreme heat of Libya and cold of Scythia which serve to make Italian herding seem more idyllic, and this contrast is reinforced in the grim account of the onset of plague in remote Noricum, a narrative based on the human plague which ends Lucretius' poem. Two vignettes bring out the horror of this epidemic in terms of Virgil's own values of work and devotion to the gods: the sacrificial animal that dies at the altar leaving unrecognizably diseased entrails (lines 483–93, cf. lines 532–3), and the ox that collapses and dies under the yoke (lines 515–30), despite its hardy innocence of human indulgence. Without their oxen men are reduced to scrabbling in the earth, while the polluted hides and fleeces represent both hideous contagion and the power of evil spirits.[22]

Book Four

Book 3 ends in horror, but the fourth book will ascend gradually from the paradox of its prologue, whose 'humble theme' is also a whole society of 'leaders great of heart, its customs, character, and conflicts' (line 4). The farmer is instructed on how to create the bees' home and environment and handle their civil wars and migrations—the affinity with human societies is at its strongest when Virgil warns his beekeeper how to choose from rival leaders, and destroy the unworthy pretender (lines 88–99).

---

[22] Lucretius seems to have ended his poem with his version of the Thucydidean plague of Athens (Thuc. 2.48–56). Virgil transfers many details to the sufferings of animals and makes an equally sudden ending to his third book.

Unlike the birds foretelling storms, Virgil's bees are seen as inspired by Jupiter (line 149) with a selfless subordination to the common good, which ensures that though the individual may die the race survives: 'their ancestral rolls include grandfathers of their fathers' (line 209). The poet even quotes sympathetically the idea that the bees are inspired, as the whole world is permeated by divine guidance, and instead of death those who perish are reabsorbed and soar to live (like Stoic heroes) among the stars (lines 220–27). But a more realistic mention of sickness leads into Virgil's most marvellous and incredible claim—that a swarm can be reborn by the magic ritual taught by Aristaeus the first beekeeper, and still practised in exotic Egypt (lines 281–94).[23] A physical account of the way Egyptians generate bees from a slaughtered bullock leads from didactic into epic and mythological narrative, by means of an appeal to the Muses to tell the origin of the miracle.

Scholarly tradition claimed that Virgil had originally given over the end of his poem to praises of his older friend Cornelius Gallus, governor of Egypt, and had been obliged to change his poem when Gallus offended Octavian and was disgraced. There could have been some lines honouring Gallus where Virgil introduces Egypt and its great river and peoples, but it is far more likely that there was no rewriting, and we have inherited the *Georgics* essentially unchanged. The double myth of loss, Aristaeus' loss of his bees and Orpheus' repeated loss of Eurydice (first when she was bitten by a snake while running away from Aristaeus, then on their failed return from Hades) has been interpreted in many ways. Aristaeus may strike the modern reader as self-pitying and without initiative in contrast with Orpheus, who braved the underworld and—in versions prior to Virgil—was able to bring back his beloved wife.[24] In an important discussion G. B. Conte has brought out the affinities which link the two

---

[23] Varro mentions incidentally at 3.16.4 that bees can be generated from a rotting bull carcass, quoting two Hellenistic lines of epigram.

[24] C. G. Perkell, *The Poet's Truth: A Study of the Poet in Virgil's Georgics* (Berkeley, 1989) notes that Virgil's contemporary Diodorus Siculus (4.15) made Orpheus successful in restoring Eurydice: there is no previous tradition of his failure.

stories.[25] Although Virgil's Hellenistic narrative form seems to subordinate the Orpheus story to that of Aristaeus (whose irresponsible attempt to rape Eurydice set off this tragic sequence), the two heroes' parallel situations give them equal significance. Both men have earned heroic stature by their achievements (as farmer, as poet), both have suffered a major loss, both attempt a testing ordeal involving a journey outside the normal world of men (underwater, under earth), but one succeeds, the other fails. Aristaeus earns his success by his devotion (and inventiveness) as a husbandman, but also by his perseverance in the battle with the supernatural shapeshifter Proteus, and obedience to his mother's instruction, an obedience which is reinforced by Virgil's apparent repetition of Cyrene's instructions from lines 531–48 at 548–51. This obedience and endurance make him both a model for the recipient of didactic poetry and a model for the farmer. Orpheus, on the other hand, has narrowed his poetry to the self-regarding lament of the elegist, which alienates him from the community. Yet Virgil has given all his emotional power to Orpheus' loving lamentation that outlives its poet beyond his own brutal death at the hands of bacchantes.

Both the Aristaeus narrative and the journey of Orpheus to the underworld are Catullan, in the fantasy and beauty of Cyrene's world under water and the poignancy of Orpheus' pleas that summon the dead, but the framework of Aristaeus' assault on Proteus is virtually unchanged from the Homeric account of Menelaus' capture of Proteus in order to discover his way home from Egypt.[26] So how is it that Virgil's Proteus has just returned to Pallene in Thrace from Carpathos? This suggests the influence of still another Greek source unknown to us; certainly a line of Callimachus' *Aitia* associated the old man of the sea with Pallene. This narrative—far from the scientific and didactic tradition— looks both backward to the new kind of miniature epic like Catullus 64, and forward to the *Aeneid*, where the first book

---

[25] See *Enciclopedia Virgiliana*, vol. i, s.v. 'Aristeo', and 'Aristaeus, Orpheus and the Georgics', in Conte, *Virgil: The Poetry of Pathos* (Oxford, forthcoming).

[26] *Odyssey* 4.351–570.

contains many echoes of Virgil's bee community in the account of
the new colony of Carthage, and the sixth book offers another,
much fuller, descent to the underworld, and similar treatment of
the dead.

As Wilkinson showed in his still definitive study,[27] the *Georgics*
have remained the least read of Virgil's poetry, and the work
which is best known from passages that are actually extraneous to
his formal theme. His contemporaries Tibullus and Horace may
well have been moved by the poem to genuine or ironic sentiment
over the countryside. Was the moneylender Alfius of *Epode* 2 a
parody of the uncomprehending reception given to the poem by
worldly readers? Agronomists took the poem seriously, although
Pliny makes specific criticisms and Columella modestly offers as
his tenth book the garden poem which Virgil 'did not have time to
write'. Those who have admired and used the poem were either
landowners or moralists (or both) like Seneca, who cites it for its
comments on human failure, and Montaigne, who found it more
perfect than the *Aeneid*: after its translation by the admiring
professional poet and critic Dryden, the *Georgics* were both read
and imitated in eighteenth-century England—though few of us
now read Thomson's *The Seasons*. But the poem was also studied
even in the brutal farming conditions of pioneer Nebraska, if the
narrator of Willa Cather's *My Ántonia* stands for his author. He
first reads the *Georgics* while studying at university, and is moved
first and foremost by those sad lines of Book 3, 'the best days of
our lives | are first to fly' (lines 66–7), but he appreciates the
creative spirit in which Virgil expressed a hope, at once bold and
devoutly humble, to bring the Muse to his own little country, to
his father's fields 'sloping down to the river and to the old beech
trees with broken tops'.[28]

Peter Fallon is both a poet and a farmer, and every line of his
translation is vivid with the sights and sounds of the countryside.

[27] L. P. Wilkinson, *The Georgics of Virgil: A Critical Survey* (Cambridge, 1969),
ch. 10, 'The Georgics in After Times'.
[28] This is Cather's version (*My Ántonia*, book 3, ch. 2) of the lines from *Eclogue* 9,
quoted above in Guy Lee's translation.

In the past it was relatively easy for students of the Roman world to read the *Georgics* with less awareness of real country life than of lofty moral and political allusions. These too are in Virgil's poem, but it is through concentration on its actual landscape and seasonal chores, its plants and creatures to be lovingly tended, that we shall come to understand and value this poetry of the land.

TRANSLATOR'S NOTE

A poem is a translation of something experienced or imagined. To *read* a poem is, further, to translate it, and the attempt to *translate* poetry involves a way of reading one poem with the hope of constructing or creating another. That act of reading depends on an affinity between one author and another, one world and another. Such translation is the fruit of various languages—the original author's, the translator's, and—if it's a translation from the past—the languages of both times and cultures. Ideally, the translation of a poem by a poet displays attributes consonant with the kind of poems he or she composes.

My partiality towards the *Georgics* hinged on more than the fact that, as Elaine Fantham records in her introduction, Virgil's home place in northern Italy had been, until a century before his birth, inhabited by Celtic tribes. I hovered round it like a bee for years, attracted to its theme of work and the satisfactions and returns of effort. I loved the poetry of this hymn to peace and people. Virgil's plea for the restoration of traditions and the re-establishment of the essential value of agricultural life accorded with my own coming to consciousness on a farm in County Meath and subsequent engagement in farming at my home nearby in the north midlands of Ireland. While my country struggled to discover new ways to evolve in the tender aftermath of 'Troubles', Virgil's delineation of the griefs and glories of a land in which people tried to found their lives, while their days were adumbrated by a civil war, was a touchstone. I cherished Virgil's moral force and how he infused his descriptions of a way of life with prescriptions of a way to live.

I resisted my first impulses to translate the poem, thinking it beyond me. Then I remembered Coleridge's observation that not all of a long poem is poetry—and I wondered if I might excerpt the more attractive, self-contained passages. My first forays were rhymed and regular in length and rhythm. But later, when I braced myself to tackle all four books, I realized that I could not

sustain those patterns. I substituted assonance for end rhymes
and let a longer line unfold. I adopted the iambic foot for its tonic
stress and employed units of pentameter. I found, however, in
this day and age, the straitjacket of a fixed form inadequate for
the variety of Virgil's invocations of divine assistance and the
direct evenness of his practical advice, for the plain song of his
care for crops, livestock, and bees (his emblem of a good society),
and the tragic opera of his recountings of the losses suffered by
Aristaeus and, twice, by Orpheus. Such variety, between what can
be predicted and what is unpredictable, nowadays invites more
than one language.

I've described elsewhere[1] the manner in which I came to feel
I'd become bilingual in English. On the one hand, there was an
idiom I inherited or absorbed by the osmosis of childhood, that
I simply *knew* by listening. On the other, there was a set of
references I'd been attracted to and studied at boarding schools
and university, and that I *learned*. Inevitably, I suppose, my trans-
formation and translocation of the poem draws on both linguistic
stores and interests. I've tried to play variations on them both to
reflect the *Georgics'* modulations between tracts of documentary
material and interludes of heightened drama.

Occasionally I came on references I didn't understand (the
roasting of red crabs, 4.48), and I resisted the temptation to
'correct' passages in which I think Virgil was mistaken—the
claim that bees take on pebbles as ballast to ground their flights
(4.194–6), the description of a certain quality of soil as ideal
(2.250). I turned a blind eye to apparent contradictions about the
advantages of letting land lie fallow.

Allen Tate spoke of the translator's 'sieve', conjuring images of
what has been let go, or lost, and what has been preserved. A
translator might, therefore, be one who pans for precious
minerals. His work aspires to 'take off', as in imitation of another
(without parodic meanness), and another take off, that uplift into
lyric flight. It is a rendering, as in provision of help or a service,
or a melting down to clarify, or a processing to extract what's still

[1] 'Afterwords', *The Georgics of Virgil* (Oldcastle, 2004).

usable, and another rendering, as in a performance. It should also be a *sur*rendering.

Ultimately, the translator's aim should be to honour the original. I learned along the way I also harboured hopes that I might inscribe the biography of one place in another age.

I owe grateful thanks to friends for the generosity of their encouragements, instructive readings, and responses: Brian Friel, Eamon Grennan, Seamus Heaney, Cormac Kinsella, Andrew McNeillie, Bernard O'Donoghue, Dennis O'Driscoll, and Justin Quinn. Further acknowledgements and gratitude are due to Ed Downe and Des Lally at Ballynahinch, and to Jean, Alice, and Adam.

The text I worked from was edited by R. A. B. Mynors (Oxford, 1969) in which he notes the absence of line 338 in Book 4. We are fortunate when we find a guide who earns our trust. His magisterial commentary (1990) led me by the hand through murky depths. I found further help in translations by John Conington, in prose (Longman Green, 1882); L. P. Wilkinson (Penguin, 1982), whose critical survey, *The Georgics of Virgil* (Cambridge, 1989) was a godsend; and C. Day Lewis (Jonathan Cape, 1940) who also 'sang in time of war the arts of peace'.

SELECT BIBLIOGRAPHY

Texts and Commentary

Mynors, R. A. B., *Virgil: Georgics* (Oxford, 1990).
Thomas, R. F., *Virgil: Georgics*, 2 vols. (Cambridge, 1988).

For those who read Latin, the commentaries of both Thomas and Mynors are indispensable. Mynors was himself a landowner who planted and maintained his own woodland and Thomas shares his deep love of trees.

General Background

Varro, *De re rustica*, and Cato, *De agri cultura*, trans. W. D. Hooper and H. B. Ash, Loeb Classical Library (Cambridge, Mass., 1936).
Frayn, J., *Subsistence Farming in Rome and Italy* (London, 1979).
Garnsey, P. D., *Cambridge Ancient History*, vol. xi (Cambridge, 1995), ch. 23, 'Crop and Climate', especially sections i–ii, offers a compact and expert survey of Italian conditions.
White, K. D., *Roman Farming* (Ithaca, NY, 1970) is a comprehensive introduction.

Critical Studies

Conte, G. B., 'Proems in the Middle', *Yale Classical Studies*, 29 (1992), 147–59.
—— 'Aristaeus, Orpheus and the Fourth Georgic', in Sarah Spence (ed.), *Poets and Critics Read Virgil* (New Haven, 2001).
Dalzell, A., *The Criticism of Didactic Poetry: Essays on Lucretius, Virgil and Ovid* (Toronto, 1998).
Farrell, J., *Virgil's Georgics and the Tradition of Ancient Epic: The Art of Allusion in Literary History* (Oxford, 1991).
Gale, M., *Virgil on the Nature of Things* (Oxford, 1999).
Griffin, J., 'The Fourth Georgic and Rome', in id., *Latin Poets and Roman Life* (London, 1985).
Klingner, F., *Virgils Georgica* (Zurich, 1963).
Miles, G., *Virgil's Georgics: A New Interpretation* (Berkeley, 1980).
Morgan, L., *Patterns of Redemption in Virgil's Georgics* (Cambridge, 1999).

Perkell, C. G., *The Poet's Truth: A Study of the Poet in Virgil's Georgics* (Berkeley, 1989).

Putnam, M., *Virgil's Poem of the Earth* (Cambridge, Mass., 1979).

Ross, D., *Virgil's Elements: Physics and Poetry in the Georgics* (Princeton, 1987).

Thomas, R. F., *Reading Virgil and his Texts: Studies in Intertextuality* (Ann Arbor, 2000). This volume gathers a number of his important articles on the *Georgics* since 1982.

Veyne, P., 'L'Histoire agraire et la biographie de Virgile dans les Bucoliques I et IX', *Revue de Philologie*, 1980, 233–57.

Volk, K., *The Poetics of Latin Didactic: Lucretius, Vergil, Ovid, Manilius* (Oxford, 2002).

Wilkinson, L. P., *The Georgics of Virgil: A Critical Survey* (Cambridge, 1969).

—— 'Virgil's Theodicy', *CQ* 13 (1963), 73–84.

Further Reading in Oxford World's Classics

Hesiod, *Theogony and Works and Days*, trans. M. L. West.

Lucretius, *On the Nature of the Universe*, trans. Ronald Melville, ed. Don Fowler and Peta Fowler.

Virgil, *The Aeneid*, trans. C. Day Lewis, ed. Jasper Griffin.

—— *The Eclogues and Georgics*, trans. C. Day Lewis, ed. R. O. A. M. Lyne.

A CHRONOLOGY OF VIRGIL

All dates are BCE.

70 Crassus and Pompey consuls: Virgil born 15 October at Andes near Mantua.

55 Crassus and Pompey consuls for second time. Virgil comes of age; goes away to study at Milan and Rome.

49 Civil war breaks out; Caesar occupies Italy, has himself elected dictator at Rome. Pompey and Republican forces evacuate to Epirus, followed by Caesar. (It is likely that Virgil withdrew to the neutral safety of Naples now if not earlier, to avoid fighting and to study philosophy. We do not know when he returned to live in Rome.)

48 Caesar defeats Pompey and Republicans at Pharsalus; Pompey assassinated by Egyptian king. Caesar in Egypt until 47.

44 15 March: assassination of Caesar. Octavian declared his heir, supported by the Senate against Mark Antony.

43 'Second' triumvirate of Octavian, Antony, and Lepidus.

42 Octavian and Antony defeat Brutus and Cassius at Philippi.

41 Octavian besieges and sacks Perusia, held by supporters of Antony, and begins confiscation of land from northern cities to settle his veterans.

40 Virgil's 4th Eclogue honours Pollio's consulship. (The book of *Eclogues* took three years to write but was complete before 35. During these years Virgil was befriended by Maecenas, and given a house on the Esquiline: he probably spent more time at Rome from now on.)

36 Octavian defeats Sextus Pompeius at Naulochus.

35 *Georgics* begun this year; the work takes Virgil seven years.

31 Octavian defeats Mark Antony and Cleopatra at Actium.

30 1 August: Octavian occupies Alexandria.

29 *Georgics* completed: read by Virgil to the returning Octavian. Virgil must have begun the *Aeneid* now if not earlier: it is reported to have taken him eleven years.

27 Octavian returns formal control of Republic to Senate and is given the title 'Augustus'. (During this decade the critic Caecilius Epirota began to give young men formal instruction in Virgil's poetry along with the work of the New Poets of Catullus' circle.)

23 Virgil reads *Aeneid* 2, 4, and 6 to Augustus and his sister Octavia after the death of her son Marcellus.

19 Virgil travels to Greece, falls ill while returning with Augustus, and dies at Brundisium. (The *Aeneid*, which he had wanted to destroy as unfinished, was published at an unknown date by order of Augustus, possibly edited by his friends Varius and Tucca.)

GEORGICS

BOOK ONE

What tickles the corn to laugh out loud, and by what star
to steer the plough, and how to train the vine to elms,
good management of flocks and herds, the expertise bees need
to thrive—my lord, Maecenas, such are the makings of the song
I take upon myself to sing.
                              Sirs of sky,
grand marshals of the firmament,
O Liber of fertility, and Ceres, our sustaining queen,
by your kind-heartedness Earth traded acorns of Epirus
for ample ears of corn and laced spring water with new wine;
and you, O Fauns, presiding lights of farming folk   10
(come dance, O Fauns, and maiden Dryads,
your gifts I celebrate as well); and you, Neptune, whose trident's
booming tap on rock first fanfared to bring forth a snorting
        horse;
and you, patron of shady woods, whose many hundred head of
        cattle
fatten, pristine, in the chaparral of Ceos;
and you too, Pan, abandoning your native groves and glades of
        Lycaeus,
caretaker of the flocks, if Maenalus means anything at all to you,
come to me, O god of Tegea,* a friend and comforter; and you,
        Minerva,
who first discovered olives; and that youth, too, creator of the
        crooked plough;*
Sylvanus, too, who carries on his back a sturdy cypress, ripped   20
        up from the roots—
a god or goddess each of you, whose care and concern is
for land, who nurtures crops not grown from seed,
and who dispatches onto plantings heavy showers from the
        heavens;
and I address you too, O Caesar,* although none knows the
        gathering of gods

in which you soon will be accommodated, or whether you would
        choose
to oversee the city or be in charge of countryside, nor knows if
        the wide world
will come to honour you as begetter of the harvest or as master
        of the seasons
(around your brow already a garland of your mother's myrtle),
or whether you will come as lord of endless sea, and seafarers
        will worship you,
30 your power alone, and the ends of earth bow to you in
        homage,
and Tethys forfeits all her waves to have you as a son-in-law,*
or whether you will add a new star to the zodiac* to quicken
        months
where there's a lull between Virgo and Libra which comes
        after it
(already ardent Scorpio contracts its claws for you
and allots to you more than your fair share of sky).
Whatever you will be (let not the nether world of Tartarus hope
        to have you
as its king, nor ever such a dread ambition lord over you,
however much Greece knows the wonders of Elysian fields
and Proserpina pays her mother little heed although she hears
        her calling her*),
40 grant me an easy course, and bless the boldness of this
        undertaking—
who shares my sympathy for countrymen whose lives are
        wanderings in the dark—
look forward now, expert already in the ways to answer our
        entreaties.

Come the sweet o' the year, when streams begin to melt and
        tumble down the hoary hills
and clods to crumble underneath the current of west winds,
it's time again to put the bull before the deep-pointed plough to
        pull his weight
and have the share glisten, burnished by the broken sod.

There's the crop, which twice has felt a touch of snow and twice
    of frosty weather,
that is a beggared farmer's prayer come true.
That's the one to fill his sheds until they're fit to burst.
And yet before we take our implements to unfamiliar   50
    territory
we must work to ascertain its changing weather and winds'
    moods,
to learn the ways and habits of that locality—
what's bound to flourish there, and what to fail.
For here you'll find a crop of grain, and there grapes growing in
    thick clusters,
and over yonder young trees thriving and grasses coming into
    green all on their own.
    Can't you see how scented saffron comes from the uplands of
      Lydia,
ivory from India, incense from soft-hearted races of Arabia;
and we get iron from unclothed inhabitants of Pontus, slimy
    castor from the Black Sea,
and the choice of mares for breeding from a region in north
    Greece?
Right from time's beginning, nature assigned these laws to last   60
    for ever,
each in its specific place, fixed such compacts from the moment
Deucalion cast onto the world the stones from which mankind
originated, a hardy race!*
                And so onward!
From the sun's first tender touch, run your mighty teams
through fertile fields, tossing sods about
for baking heat to break them down to dust.
But if you've not got high yielding soil you will do well
to rake it with a shallow sock by the shine of that time's
    brightest star,
to ensure either that weeds won't block the way for wholesome
    crops
or that a bare sandy plot retains whatever moisture's there.   70
    Take turns to let the land lie fallow after it's been harvested,

let fields left to themselves recuperate and renew themselves
     with firmer footing
or, with a switch of season, set down, say, tawny emmer or
     einkorn,
where once you'd gathered an outpour of pulses
with their rustling pods, or drawn spindly vetch
and bitter lupins' brittle stalks and susurrating stems.
For it's a fact and true, a crop of flax will parch a place,
as will wild oats, as will a sprawl of poppies doused in their
     forgetfulness.
That said, you'll lighten loads of routine by rotation.
80 Don't spare dry land its fill of dung,
don't hesitate to spread a heap of grimy ashes on spent fields.
While your land gets a chance to rest by changing crops
don't think that all the while your fallow isn't earning a
     return.
    Frequently there's much to gain by setting flame to idle acres
and letting their thin stubble burn—either because it helps
engender some weird force and rich feed for the soil
or because the fire scalds all its faults and failings
and sweats out baleful moisture.
Or is it that the heightened heat unclogs the pores and opens
     passages
90 through which the sap ascends into new shoots
or makes clay even firmer by closing yawning waterways
so that it isn't blasted by a fall of rain or sun's excessive benison
or the bite of freezing winds that batter from the north?
    And as for that, great is the good he does a field who with a
     mattock breaks apart
its lumps and clumps, then with a wicker hurdle harrows it,
earning a look he likes from Ceres high on her Olympian heights,
just as he contributes much who raises flat land into ridges
by ploughing one way, then cross-ploughing,
and regularly works his lands and keeps a tight rein on his
     holding.
100   The countryman should pray for wet summers and mild
     winters;

corn delights in hiemal dust. Then the country's in good heart—
there's nothing brings out better in places such as Mysia,
and Gargarus* can be amazed by its own harvests.

    Need I single him for praise who follows
hard on the heels of setting seed by crumbling heaps of
        unreceptive soil
and steering into tracks streams to irrigate the plantings?
And when the countryside's aglow and all that grows is
        withering in the heat
see how he conjures water from the brim to spill downhill in
        sloping channels,
a flow that grumbles over gravel, gushing onward
to allay the thirst of scorched places.   110
Or indeed the one who, to ensure that stalks won't lodge
        beneath
the weight of ears, grazes to the ground the tender shoots
that grow in such profusion as soon as they clear the furrow's
        ridge,
or that one who drains swamp-gathers in a soak-pit,
especially in the course of those unsettled months when rivers
        burst
their banks and smear mudspills everywhere on everything,
causing steam to rise again from hollows.

    And don't imagine that, for all the efforts and exertions—
man's and beast's—to keep the sod turned over, there's not a
        threat
from plagues of geese, or Strymon cranes, from bitter roots of   120
        chicory,
nor hurt or harm in shade of trees. For it was Jupiter himself
who willed the ways of husbandry be ones not spared of trouble
and it was he who first, through human skill, broke open land, at
        pains
to sharpen wits of men and so prevent his own domain being
        buried
in bone idleness. No settler tamed the plains before our Father
        held his sway
and it was still against the law to stake a claim to part of them.

Men worked towards the common good and the earth herself,
unbidden, was lavish in all she produced.
And it was he who instilled in snakes their deadly poison,
130 bade wolves to prowl, and seas to surge.
He shook down honey from the leaves and had all fires
     quenched.
He stopped the flow of wine that coursed rampant in the rivers
so that by careful thought and deed you'd hone them bit by bit,
those skills, to coax from furrows blades of corn
and spark shy flame from veins of flint.

     That was the first time ever hollowed alders sailed on water,
and seagoing men began to number, and then name, the stars—
the Pleiades, the Hyades, and Lycaon's child, the glittering
     Great Bear.
Then men came up with ways to try to trap wild animals, by
     setting snares
140 of sticky sticks for birds and rounding game in glades with packs
     of hunting hounds.
And by this time someone was dragging rivers with a net,
plumbing their depths; another trawled the open sea with his
     soaking mesh.
Then came tempered iron and the saw-blade's rasping rhythm
(for earlier man was wont to split his wood with wedges).
All this before the knowledge and know-how which ensued.
Hard work prevailed, hard work and pressing poverty.

     It was Ceres who first taught to men the use of iron ploughs—
that time wild strawberries and oak berries were scanty in the
     sacred groves
and Dodona* was miserly with her support.
150 Soon growing grain grew into harder work.
Blight rusted stalks, and thistles mustered into view to lord it
     over
all that you accomplished; crops began to flounder, a rough
     growth to advance—
goosegrass, or 'cleavers', and bristling burrs—while wild oats
and dreaded darnel ruled head and shoulder over your well-
     tended plot.

So, unless you're set to spend the whole day hoeing weeds,
and making noise to scare off birds, and slashing back with
    hooks
the branches darkening the lands, and all your prayers for rain
    are answered,
alas, my friend, heaps of grain next door will stare you in the
    face
and you'll be raiding oaks for acorns to ease the ache of hunger.

Now let me tell about the tools and tackle unflagging farmers   160
    had to have
in their arsenal, for none has sowed or saved a crop without
    them.
The ploughshare first, and the curved plough's solid board,
and Ceres' hefty carts for sheaves,
threshing rakes and sledges, and the heavy-weighted mattock.
And then the lighter implements of wickerwork—arbutus
    gates and hurdles,
and Iacchus' marvellous riddle* which serves to sort the chaff
    from grain.
So think ahead—stockpile a cache of these in time
if you're to earn the satisfactions of that heavenly estate.
    To make the plough's main curve, fashion by force
a pliant elm while it's still growing in the ground.   170
Then to its stock fit and fasten an eight-foot pole,
earth-timbers, and a twin-backed beam.
Light lime you will have kept aside to make the yoke,
and for the tiller a length of beech to steer it from behind.
Hung in the hearth, smoke will season wood components.

I could, if I'd not seen you back away from such concerns,
regale you with a store of ancient learning.
To begin: grade the threshing floor with the heavy roller,
taking pains to tamp it tight with chalk
so that no growth breaks through and it holds firm and doesn't   180
    crumble.
Let no blights of pests or parasites squat there;

for often, underground, the mouse sets up his house and home
and the groping mole excavates a bolt-hole
and you come upon a shrew or fieldmouse in a hollow
and other creatures earth turns out—the beetle scurries
to spoil heaps of wheat, the emmet hurries to safeguard against
  a want some rainy day.
 And so pay close attention when stands of walnut trees
disport themselves with blossoms and their fragrant boughs
  bend down—
if they produce abundant fruit, your corn crop will be bountiful,
190 great heat will follow and guarantee your harvest.
But if, instead, a luxury of leaves abounds and throws a shadow
  over everything,
you'll waste a world of time at grinding, end up all chaff and
  little grain.
I've seen with my own eyes plantsmen steeping seeds
before they set them down, drenching them in saltpetre and the
  dregs of olive oil,
so that their deceiving pods would grow a greater yield,
one that might amount to something over a low flame.
 And I have seen long-tried and-tested crops begin to fail
where no one took the time each year to sort and save
the finest grain, seed by seed. For that's the way it is—
200 world forces all things to the bad, to founder and to fall,
just as a paddler in his cot struggling to make headway up a
  river,
if he lets up a minute, will find himself
rushed headlong back between the banks.

What's more, you need to keep a weather eye on sky
  formations*—
such as Arcturus, the twin kids of the Charioteer, or Draco, that
  bright light,
and stay vigilant as those mariners who, homeward bound, ride
  stormy seas,
yet venture close to Pontus, the Straits of Abydos and their
  oyster beds.

And when September's equinox doles to day as many hours as
 to night
and splits the world in two fair halves, both equal light and
 dark,
then set to work the oxen, men, broadcast barley in the fields, 210
until midwinter's whelming showers slap you in the face.
Then, too, it's time to plant linseed and seeds of poppies (loved
 by Ceres),
time to tie yourself to the plough while the still-dry earth
accepts it and the settled weather lingers.
 Set beans in springtime, the time alfalfa happens in collapsing
 furrows,
and millet clamours for its annual attention,
when Taurus, gilt-horned and incandescent, gets the new year
up and running, and the Dog succumbs to his advance.
But if you've been working towards a strong output of wheat
or you're heartset on hardy ears of corn, 220
hold off until one of the Seven Sisters steals away from you at
 dawn
and the Star of Knossos, the shining Northern Crown, retires
before you entrust to the ground seed you've pledged
and invest in soil that couldn't keep its promise to repay the
 hopes of a whole year.
Some cropsmen thought that they could not delay till May
 began to wane
and the crops that they were counting on jeered them with
 hollow heads of oats.
 But if you're the kind who's satisfied with sowing seeds of
 vetch and tares
and second-rate green beans and don't look down even on
 Egyptian pulses,
you won't mistake in any way the signs a setting Boötes
 transmits—
you might as well get on with it, and carry on your sowing until 230
 you're up to here in frosts!
 This is the very reason the sun god is so faithful to his path
between each of the dozen fixed divisions of his orbit.

Five spheres make up the heavens,* of which one, and only one,
is always blushing brightly and always flushed by his flaming
     fire.
And all around, left and right, a cyanic realm stretches far as far
     can be,
hard frosts and ice and gloomy spills.
Between this and the middle sphere a pair of zones is given
by godly grace to pitiful man, through both of which a way's
     laid down
and the series of signs takes turns along their roundabout way.
240 And the universe, just as it rises to the lofty slopes of the
     Riphaean ranges,
pitches downward in the south, in Africa.
There's a pole that always looms above us, while its counterpart
lies underfoot* in Stygian dark and the infernal shades.
Here the sky's enormous serpent slithers in and out,
the image of a river, between the Big and Little Dipper,*
those constellations that disdain to be touched or tainted by
     Atlantic's waters.
     There, or so they say, either it's the dead of night and so
         still—
a black shadow stretching over everything as if for ever—
or dawn comes back to them on its way back from us, daylight's
     chaperone,
250 and, when morning first inspires us with its puffing horses,
there the lamps of evening are coming on, and glow.

And so we have the power to anticipate uncertain weather—
the day to reap, the day to sow—
and when the time is right to plunge our oars into
untrustworthy seas, when to launch an armed armada,
when's best, even, to fell a pine tree in the forest.
     It's not for nothing we keep an eye on sky for signs
that come and go, or on the year's four equal parts.
Say the farmer's grounded by a cold snap's burst of rain,
260 he'll seize the time for odd jobs he'd be rushing when it's fine.
The ploughman points the blunted share with hammer blows

or gouges troughs from trees,
or brands the herds, or checks the stocks of grain;
another whittles stakes and twin-pronged forks
and readies sally switches to tie the dangling vine.
And now might be the time to weave fruit baskets out of
    brambly branches
or roast the corn beside the fire before you crush it with the
    quern.
  For it's a fact, on holidays you're actually allowed by gods'
    laws and by men's
to attend to certain labours—so let no scruple deflect you
if you would clear a drain, or fill a gap around the cornfield,   270
set traps for birds or fire to briars,
and dip the whole flock in the flow to stave off scab.
These are the times the farmer weighs the little donkey
down with creels of olive oil and fruit he's picked
and comes back later from the town with a grinding stone or a
    supply of pitch.
  The moon herself prescribed days suitable for certain
    work.*
Beware the fifth, the day on which grim Death
was born, as were the Furies, the day the Earth whelped ghastly
    giants—
Coeus, Iapetus, and restless Typhoeus—and another heinous
    brood,
the brothers who conspired to bring down the very heavens.   280
Three times did they essay to heap Mount Ossa on Mount
    Pelion,
and then—it followed—to impose on Ossa Olympus' leafy
    heights.
And three times he, the Father himself, blasted those piled hills
    with lightning.
  The seventeenth's a lucky day for laying down the vine,
for rounding up and breaking in an ox or heifer, for setting up
    the loom.
The ninth day smiles on anyone who runs away, but frowns on
    those who steal.

It's true, the small small hours are best for many things,
or that very moment the sun is fledging and the land's still
    dabbed with dew.
Night's the best for cutting lighter crops, night's best for well-
    drained meadows,
290 for then there is no lack of lingering moisture.

There's a certain sort of man who by winter firelight
stays up all night edging iron implements.
And all the while, with soothing songs lightening the load of her
    routine,
his helpmeet runs across her loom her rattling reed,
and in the hearth a flame reduces the sweet-scented must,
its bubbles simmering in a pot she skims with brush-strokes of
    broad leaves.
While, on the other hand, in midday's highest heat, you're
    better off
knocking red or ruddy grain or bruising parched produce on the
    threshing floor.
Plough on days you'd strip to the waist; sow the same.
300 Winter's the time for farmers to unwind. In colder months
countrymen enjoy themselves, taking turns to entertain.
Congenial winter is a treat: it banishes their woes and worries,
as if a laden ship just docked in a safe haven
and sailors had begun to decorate its stern with garlands.
Still and all, that season has its labours, they file away the
    hours—
the gather-up of acorns, bayberries and olive-berries, and the
    purple berries of the myrtle.
What's more, it's time for you to set out traps for herons, cast
    nets for stags,
to course the long-lugged hare and fell a hind
by hurling your coarse hempen slings the way they do in the
    Balearics—
310 all this while snow falls from the heavens, and floods advance
    their loads of ice.
What can I tell about the storms of autumn and its signs,

or, even, when the days are closing down and summer sun's
    abating,
what then must men beware of? Or, say, when spring comes
    tumbling
down in showers and crops of corn are tall already,
their green stalks standing proud with sap?
How often I have seen, just as the farmer's driven in to reap
the flaxen field and top the fragile barley crop,
the clash of squalls and gales in battle mode
as they ripped up from roots the swathes of ripe and ready corn
and held them up, the way malefic whirlwinds   320
toss beardless stalks around the place, hither and yon.

    At other times a rush of water cascades from the sky,
clouds spill their mass into the foul darkness of a deluge,
as the heavens open and the rainfall wipes the smiles
off the faces of the crop the oxen worked so hard to make.
Ditches fill to the brim, rampant channels overflow,
the sea rampaging up each boiling inlet.

    Then Jupiter, squire of the sky, straddling the night clouds,
    dispatches
from his gleaming hand a thunderbolt and makes the whole
    world quake.
Wild beasts take off, and everywhere human hearts   330
are laid low in a panic. He hurls that blazing dart
onto Athos, Rhodope, and the peaks of Ceraunia;*
south winds redouble and rains intensify;
now the great groves in the gale, and now the shores, burst into
    tears.
So, in apprehension, keep an eye on each month's
    constellations,
and note where the cold star of Saturn steals away to,
and in which orbits the planet Mercury is wandering.
Above all else, venerate the gods and pay your yearly offerings
to Ceres, when the grass is in good heart,
at the very end of winter when spring brings on clear skies.   340
Then lambs are fit, wine's at its best.
Sleep's pure delight, and on the heights deep shadows lie.

Have all your workers be worshippers of that goddess,
and offer milk and honey and mild wine,
and march a victim three times around fresh crops for luck
while all the others celebrate, a band of allies in support.
Let them implore her loudly to come and rest with them,
but stay the hand of anyone who'd lay a sickle to a single ear of
      corn
who has not wreathed his head with oak leaves in her honour
350 and made up dances and sung hymns to her.
    And so that we might be prepared to read unerring clues—
anticipate heatwaves and showers and winds precipitating
      cold—
he himself, the Father, decreed what each moon phase
would mean, the sign by which south winds subside,
what always indicates that farmers keep their teams in stalls
and near to hand. The minute winds begin to swell
and seas to surge, a brattling sound
starts up in the mountains, chaotic noises echo
far along the coast, and murmurs in woodlands increase.
360 Then the waves are in no mood to bear a ship
and cormorants dash back from sea and bring their throaty
      roars
to the shore; waterhens more used to waterways
play on dry land—a sign for herons to forsake
the marshes and weave their way high in the sky.
And you can readily predict impending gales
by shooting stars that blaze their way through the night sky
and leave a white trail printed there.
You'll see airy chaff and fallen leaves afloat on waves,
down and feathers fluttering there.

370 But then, when from the quarters of the north wind lightning
      flashes
and from the home place of the east and west winds thunder
      rumbles,
the countryside's awash with the overwhelm of ditches
and seafarers furl their soaking sails.

A spill of rain should never catch you unawares,
for either you'll have seen soaring cranes seek protection in the
    bottoms,
a heifer face the sky suspiciously and work its nose to sniff the
    wind,
sweet-singing swallows circle round a lake,
or heard the frogs stuck in the mud and croaking their old
    grumpy sounds.
More often you'll see ants transporting eggs along a narrow,
    well-worn way
from their safest shelter, or a mighty rainbow bending down   380
to take a drink, or as they evacuate their feeding grounds
a cavalcade of squawky rooks.
    Next, a host of seabirds and those contented rummaging
in grassland swamps of Asia Minor or pools along the river
    Caÿster
mimic each other by splashing spray onto their upper bodies,
now plunging head first into waves, now spurting underwater,
so that you'd think they're revelling in the ordinary routines of
    washing.
Then a crow, strutting the deserted shore,
proclaims in its mean caw, Rain, rain, and then more rain.
    In truth, even in the dark of night, young women busy   390
    carding wool
can foretell a storm's approach: they notice in their lighted
    lamps
a sputtering, and watch spent wicks begin to clot and harden.
And it's as easy to predict sunny days and stretches of clear
    weather
in the wake of heavy showers if you're attentive to the signs.
For the points of stars won't then appear blunted
nor the moon's own beams rise up as though it borrowed light
    from her kin
nor clouds like wispy fleeces be borne across the heavens.
Along the strand, kingfishers—favourites of the sea-nymph,
    Thetis—
won't extend their wings in the warm sun

400 nor filthy lazing swine think of tossing with their snouts the
            bedding in their sties.
Instead, the clouds determine to hang heavy on the lowlands,
while, at sunfall, night's silent raptor watches from above
and wastes its time hooting charms and hexes.
High in the skies Nisus comes into view, a sparrowhawk,
and Scylla pays the price for that lock of reddish hair she stole.*
Whenever she goes flying by, splitting the heavens,
there he'll be, her father and her mortal foe, spitting screeches
and in hot pursuit; yes, where Nisus takes himself up and away
there she'll ever be, slicing heaven with her wings and cutting it
            to pieces.
410 Then ravens strain their voices to pour forth their one pure
            note, three times or four,
and, perched high on their roosts, croak from their green shade
in ways that we don't understand but with better than their
            customary cheer.
How it seems to lift their hearts, when a rain belt's hurried
            overhead,
to turn back to their new-hatched brood and their beloved
            nestlings.
Not that I accept, however hard I try, that they've the slightest
            talent given them by god
nor that fate bestowed on them any shred of ancient lore.
And yet—where there are changes in the weather and shifts in
            atmosphere—
Jupiter, the god of sky, with sodden southern winds condenses
all that had been airy and rarefies what had been so oppressive.
420 Then they have a change of heart and give themselves to
            different feelings,
different from when gusts were shaking up the clouds—
and that's the cause, across the country, of concord among birds,
of livestock lying down in peace and ravens crying out their
            hallelujahs.
    It's true—you keep your eye on the fleet-footed sun
and any run of moons, and dawn won't take you by surprise,
nor tricks of cloudless night catch you off guard.

For when the moon collects herself in brimming fires,
if she is cradling an amorphous shape and sheen you have
    'earthshine'
and spills of rain are on the way to those who hoe the fields and
    row the waves.
But if she blushes like a maiden there'll be a breeze;   430
the advent of the wind precipitates a flush on the fresh face of
    the moon.
And if, on her fourth morning (that most reliable of all),
she sallies through an open sky, her horns unblurred,
all that day long, and all the days that stem from it
until month's end, you needn't fret yourself about wind or rain,
and sailors standing safe ashore may count their blessings
and give thanks to those sea-deities, Glaucus, Panopea, and
    Ino's son, Melicertes.*
  And the sun itself, on its way up or sliding down below the
    waves,
offers signs—none more deserving of our heed than those
    attached to it
as it rises in the morning or as it meets the winking stars.   440
If he appears at dawn all stained with spots
or hides in clouds the middle of his face
watch out for heavy showers: there'll be a south wind pounding
    from on high
that is no friend to trees or crops or cattle.
But if he comes pushing through thick clouds in all directions
like bright spokes of a section of a wheel
or if the goddess of the dawn rises wanly from her consort's
    saffron couch
beware: there's nothing you can do for them, your ripe shoots of
    vines,
such heavy hail will bounce and clatter on your roof.
This, too, when he's passed through and is retiring to the   450
    heavens,
you'll do well to remember, for often we'll observe odd colours
stray across his countenance—dark blues declare
that there'll be rains, while tints of fire forecast hasky winds.

But if those hues begin to blend with glowing red
look out for gales and stormy clouds together.
On such a night, spare me the thought that anyone would
    contemplate
that he'd set sail or as much as touch the tie rope of his boat.
But if, when he presents the day and then retracts it,
his face is just as clear both times, your storm fears
460 are a thing of nothing, and you'll see trees tilting in a gentle
    northerly.
    In short, whatever evening's bringing on, whence winds
    propel
fair-weather clouds, and what wet southerlies portend,
the sun will advance warning signs. Who'd dare to question
the sun's word? For it is he, once more, who forestalls troubles,
hidden but at hand, of conflicts festering out of sight.
And it was he who felt for Rome that time that Caesar fell*
and veiled his gleaming head in gloom
so dark the infidels began to fear that night would last for ever;
although, in that catastrophe, the earth itself and stretches of
    the sea,
470 unruly hounds, and bad-natured birds, sounded their
    predictions too.
How frequently we've watched eruptions of Mount Etna
and the expulsions from her furnaces spill on the one-eyed
    giants' lands
fireballs and molten lava.
The skies of Germany resounded with the din of war,
weird stirrings caused the Alps to tremble.
What's more, in quiet groves a voice was heard by many peoples,
a monstrous voice, and pallid spectres loomed
through the dead of night and—dare I say it?—
cattle spoke. The rivers ground to a halt, gaping holes appeared,
480 and in the sanctuary carved ivories began to weep the tears of
    mourning
and bronzes to perspire. The Po, king river, swept away in
    raging rushes
across the open plains whole plantations, cattle and their stalls,

swept all away. That was a time

when entrails, carefully scrutinized, showed nothing but the
worst

and wellsprings spouted blood all day

and hill towns howled all night with wolves.

And never was a time more streaks of lightning split a limpid
sky—

nor dismal comets flared at such close intervals.

So was it any wonder that Philippi observed for the second time

the clash of Roman forces in a civil war,* 490

and gods above did not think it a shame that we, with our own
blood,

would once again enrich wide-spreading Emathia* and the
plains below Haemus.*

Nothing surer than the time will come when, in those fields,

a farmer ploughing will unearth

rough and rusted javelins and hear his heavy hoe

echo on the sides of empty helmets and stare in open-eyed
amazement

at the bones of heroes he's just happened on.

O Romulus, god of our fathers, strength of our homes, our
mother Vesta,

who watches over our Etruscan Tiber and the palaces of Rome,

stand back, don't block the way of this young one who comes to 500
save

a world in ruins. More than enough, and long ago, we paid in
blood

for the lies Laomedon told at Troy.* Long, long ago since
heaven's royal estate

begrudged you first your place among us, Caesar,

grumbling of your empathies with the cares of men and the
victories they earn.

For right and wrong are mixed up here, there's so much warring
everywhere,

evil has so many faces, and there is no regard for the labours

of the plough. Bereft of farmers, fields have run to a riot of
weeds.

Scythes and sickles have been hammered into weapons of war.
Look here, the east is up in arms; look there, hostilities in
    Germany.
510 Neighbouring cities renege on what they pledged and launch
    attacks—
the whole world's at loggerheads, a blasphemous battle,
as when, right from the ready, steady, go, chariots quicken on a
    track
until the driver hasn't a hope of holding the reins and he's
    carried away
by a team that pays heed to nothing, wildly away and no control.*

BOOK TWO

BLOCK TWO

Thus far I have been singing of working the land, and stars in
     heaven.
So now I turn to you, Bacchus, you and the thick thickets people
     think of when they think of you,
and, while I'm at it, to what the slow-growing olive gives.
Be with me now, O Patron of the vine, here where your copious
     gifts abound,
where by your grace, in every autumn, the country swells with
     your full flower
and the vintage foams to overflow the vats.
Be with me now, O Patron of the vine, tear off your buskins
and come paddling with me in this season's musty dye!

Lesson one. The ways to propagate a tree are many.
Some take root on their own, with no one's help,   10
and put themselves about the place, throughout the plains,
by river bends—the supple willow and the bendy broom,
poplars, and a copse of sallies with their silver undersides.
But others spring from seeds they've dropped, such as the
     chestnut,
or that oak whose greenery adorns the groves of Jupiter,*
and the other one* that Greeks believe can tell what is to come.
And others still whose undergrowth shoots up along the root,
the cherry and the elm, while laurels of Parnassus,*
seedlings still, shelter in their mother's shade.
These methods were first Nature's way for each and every tree   20
in woods and sacred groves to thrive and flourish.
Now there are other ways, found out by trial and error.
Some have taken slips from the parent tree's tender trunk
and landed them in trenches; some planted cuttings in a field,
their ends divided into quarters, held up by hardwood stakes.
     And there are others, forest trees, which call for layering
to come into their own at home in soil they're used to;

and others still which have no need for roots, and he who prunes
        them
doesn't have to wonder as he entrusts back to the ground a
        cutting
30 from the upper branches. Why, even when you've chopped an
        olive tree—
can you believe it?—buds burgeon from its seasoned stump.
How often have we seen the bough of one tree turned into
        another,
and none the worse for wear—the pear transformed to issue
        apples,
the plum branch blushing with its stonehard cherries?
So, come on, countrymen, and learn the character of every
        species,
make wild fruits sweeter through your care, and let no land lie
        waste.
What could proffer more reward than setting vines across the
        slopes of Ismarus
and covering the hillsides of Taburnus* with a cloak of olives?
And you, Maecenas, stand beside me now in this, the work I've
        taken on,
40 you to whom the largest fraction of my fame belongs by right,
have no second thoughts before the great adventure into which
        I've launched myself.
    Not that I could ever hope to feature all things in my verses—
not even if I had a hundred mouths, as many ways of speech,
and a voice as strong as iron. Stand by me now—as we proceed
        along the shoreline,
land close to hand. I'll waste none of your time with made-up
        rhymes,
or riddles, or prolonged preambles.
    Those trees which of their own accord rear themselves into
        the realm of light
mature unfruitful—that's a fact—though otherwise they're
        sound and strong,
and that's due to the quality of soil. And even these,
50 grafted to another or set carefully in a well-worked bed,

will outgrow their wildwood ways and with attentive care
will toe the line of what you have laid down for them.
In fact, those volunteers, sprouting from the base of trees,
will do the same, if you set them out, that is, in other spaces,
but if you don't, the parent tree's looming leaves and branches
will smother them and nip in the bud their whole ability to bear.
Indeed, that said, the tree that rears itself from windfalls
comes on half-heartedly and, preserving nought but shade for
    future generations,
its fruit will be a thing of nothing, its erstwhile flavour long
    forgotten,
and vines brought on this way bear only sorry sets of grapes,   60
    booty for birds.
   It's a fact and true—all trees cry out for work,
you'll have to train them in trenches, however trying that may be.
Olive trees fare best when grown on the trunk, vines by that
    practice
we've named layering, Paphian myrtles best from solid stems;
from slips, the healthy hazel, the mighty ash,
and the poplar out of which Hercules once made himself a
    garland,
just like the sacred oaks, the sky-high palm,
and the fir ahead of which lie disasters of the deep.
And, yes, through grafting, the shaggy strawberry dispenses
    walnuts,
and barren planes have borne a healthy pick of apples,   70
chestnut trees have sponsored beeches, and pear blossom
    whitened
manna ash, while underneath an elm sows have prospered on a
    feed of acorns.
These are not straightforward acts, grafting and implanting.
You see, when buds develop inside the bark and split its skin
a narrow pocket forms right on the knot.
To this you should affix the scion,
coaxing it to meld into the sappy rind.
But knot-free trunks you cut back all the way
and into the solid bole you etch deep wedges.

80 Next, insert those slips that are likelier to bear—and in jig time
a mighty tree is starting up to heaven, its branches jubilant,
astounded by new foliage and fruits which aren't its own.

And then you'll find there's more than one kind of elm,
and willow, and lotus tree, and the cypresses of Ida,
more than a single species of oily olive—
this comes in every shape and size and every shade of
       bitterness.
There are all sorts of apples in the orchards of Alcinous;* the
       shoot that grows
the pear from Crustumine wouldn't bear the Tarentine* nor
       those that are each one a handful.
Nor are they one and the same, the vintage grapes that drape our
       arbours,
90 as those they pick in Lesbos from the tendrils of Methymna,
or those in Thasos off the coast of Thrace, or paler breeds from
       Egypt.
Some suit a fertile soil, some a lighter sort.
Psythian makes best raisin-wine, while Lagean leaves you
       footless—just like that!—
and ties your tongue when you least expect it.
Purple grapes, or those that ripen first—and, oh, the fruit of
       Rhaetia,*
what song of mine could do you justice? Fine as you are, don't
       think yourself
the match of those stored in Falernian cellars. Aminnean wines,
       full-bodied with a long finish,
surpass that of Tmolus and even Phanae's finest, and, of course,
       the humbler Argite,
though none can rival this for its great yield
100 or all the years it lasts in prime condition.
      Don't think I would omit the wine of Rhodes, fit for gods
and saved till last, or Bumastus with its lavish clusters.
But there's no number for the sorts of wine nor names
for each of them, and little to be gained by trying to concoct
       the list.

Who'd know them all would know how many grains of sand
the west wind pitches through Saharan wastes,
how many waves* break on the Adriatic shore
when east winds smash against a fleet of ships at sea.
Not that every soil can bear all types of things.
Willows grow by river banks, alders root   110
in swampy depths, the mountain ash on stony heights.
Myrtles flourish by the shore, while—here it is—Bacchus adores
wide-open uplands, and yew a chilly northern aspect.
Turn your eyes to the ends of earth and those who till its acres—
the homes of Arabs in the east, Scythian tribes* with painted
        bodies.
Each nation has specific trees. None but the Indies grow
ebony, none but Arabia its sticks of incense.
What need is there for me—because you know already—to
        mention
fragrant resin exuded by the balsam or the pods of evergreen
        acacia?
Or the cotton fields of Ethiopia,   120
or how the Chinese* people comb silky fleeces from the leaves?
Or mention forests, contiguous to the ocean, that are another
        pride of India,
or at the last outpost of earth the trees so tall
that none could fire arrows to their tips, however hard he tries,
and there they're no mean marksmen when it comes to taking up
        the bow.
    That bitter fruit, the citron, with its aftertaste,
is a product of Media*—and there's no better help at hand
to wash the system of its toxins when,
with a mess of herbs and more malignant hexes,
a wicked stepmother spikes your drink.   130
The tree itself's a mighty one, the image of a laurel,
and, if it weren't for the discrepant scent it casts so far,
you'd argue it's a laurel. No wind can make it shed its leaves,
its blossom has a stubborn hold. The Medes use it to cure
foul odours in the mouth and treat shortness of breath in older
        people.

But neither the forests of Media, richest of lands,
nor glorious Ganges, nor even Hermus rattling with alluvial
    gold,
begin to match all that is due our praise in Italy.
                            No, nor Bactra,
    nor the Indies,
nor Arabia and all its sands opulent with incense.

140   For this is land, this land of ours, no oxen ever turned with
        ploughs,
their nostrils flaring flames, nor where a dragon's teeth were
    sown,
nor where a human harvest trembled—in ranks of helmets and
    serries of spears.*
Rather, it proliferates with produce and fine wines of Monte
    Massico;
olives abound, and bullocks in full bloom.
From here the warhorse struts across the battlefield.
From here, Clitumnus,* came the washed-white flocks and the
    bull that was
primed for the sacrifice, those animals that often bathed in your
    holy waters
and drew to the temples of the gods throngs who celebrated
    Roman triumphs.
Here it's constant spring—and summer out of season.

150 Twice cattle calve every year and twice the apple trees present
    their plenty.
    And—it must be said—there's no sign here of raging tigers or
        lions'
seed, breed, or generation, or of monkshood that tricks anyone
    unfortunate to pick it;
neither does the scaly serpent drag itself through the land
in endless circles or rear itself in threatening coils.
Think of the shining cities and the accomplishments of men,
towns created by such effort on steepling rocks
with rivers rumbling underneath their ancient walls.
Is there any need for me to mention the seas that wash above it
    and below,

or its great lakes—you, Larius, the greatest of them all,
or Benacus with crashing waves, just like a sea?   160
Is there any need for me to mention the havens and the reef's
    protection
of Lucrine,* as they aggravate the sea's resentments
where waves, repulsed, resound from far across the Sound of
    Julius
and drive Tyrrhenian tides through the channels of Avernus?
  Deep in the veins of this land silver shows, and copper mines;
its rivers run rich with gold.
Hers are the most intrepid men—fierce Marsians, and Samnite
    stock;
Ligurians, misfortune's friends; Volscian lancers*
and the Decii she produced; tribes of Marius and great
    Camillus;
the battle-hardened Scipios,* and you yourself, Caesar, first of   170
    all mankind,
you who, already champion of Asia's furthest bounds,
rebuffs the craven Indian* from the arched portals of the capital.
Hail to thee, Italy, holy mother of all that grows,
mother of men—in your honour I plunge into material and
    measures
prized in days of old, daring to divulge the hallowed sources
and sing a hymn to works and days through the towns of Rome.

Now to the quality of land in any place—what's best about it,
its tints and textures, and its capacity for produce.
First that rugged country, those mean slopes,
stony soil, shallow loam, a world of brambles—   180
a happy home for long-lived olives.
One sure sign of such a place is oleaster in profusion,
its berries veritably blanketing the ground.
  But loamy land, that holds the spills of hills and rain,
a plain enhanced with plants and grass, proud teats of growth,
the like of which we're used to seeing when we gaze
down into deep valleys (into which, from heights of cliffs, rivers
    spout

contributing the gift of mud), or high, south-facing ground
that's liable to grow the curved share's foe—that is bracken—
190 such soil will one day proffer hale and hearty vines
and plenteous wine from bulging bunches,
a flood of grape juices, such as we pour for gods from golden
goblets
as seen on altar carvings when a plump Etruscan plays his ivory
pipe
and, on straining spears, we make our offerings of steaming
entrails.
That said, if rearing calves and fattening lambs is what
you care to do, or even goats that rip the roots of all that grows,
try the wooded fields and open spaces at Tarentum
and rolling plains such as Mantua was misfortunate enough to
lose,
where graceful swans are flourishing in weedy waters.
200 There's no end there to feed and drink for stock:
what they crop in the course of one long day
dew will restore in the chill hours of one short night.
As like as not, ground that's black when it's subjected to the
share,
whose soil is friable (the sort we aim to reproduce by turning it),
that's best for corn; you'll nowhere see more waggonfuls
dragged home by struggling bullocks;
that, or lands from which a careless farmer carried timber off,
laid waste to woods that had stood tall for years on years
and wrecked the ancient habitats of birds by ripping up
210 roots and all. Their nestlings left, their mothers made for high
sky,
but those once straggly acres blossom now behind your team.
You'll get gravel in a hilly place, that scarcely serves
surfeit of lowly spurge or rosemary to feed the bees;
and riddled tufa, and chalk well worn by dour watersnakes,
make plain there is no other place supplying reptiles
with such fills of food as they prefer, nor proffering such hidey-
holes as they'd kill for.
Land that tosses off the whiffs of mist

and breathes in dew and breathes it out again at will,
and dresses always in its green attire,
and doesn't tarnish tools with rust or marks of minerals— 220
that's the land for growing vines to trail around your elms and
for big yields of olives;
give it a go—you'll find it's in good heart for grazing
or for submitting to the plough's advances.
Among all that Capua possesses, it has that kind of land to work
along the ridges of Vesuvius, and Clanius whose floods
dispeopled Acerrae.*

Listen. Here's how you'll tell the sort of soil you're dealing
with.
If it's a compact one you need, or one more porous
(one's good for corn, one for vines,
dedicate the denser one to Ceres, the looser one to Bacchus),
trust your eyes to be the judge—and order that a hole be dug 230
deep in the ground. Then backfill all the earth
and trample flat. A shortfall?—it's a light soil,
fit for herds and flocks, or healthy vines.
A surplus?—leftover land when you've refilled
the trench—and you have heavy land on hand—
all that's in store is sods and clods and awkward ridges:
prepare to break that ground with sturdy oxen.
  As for that land that brings tears to the eyes, 'bitter' land as
locals say
(inhospitable to harvests, that no amount of ploughing
sweetens),
where vines won't live up to their name and apples aren't worth 240
mentioning,
here's how you'll recognize it—reach to your reeky rafters
and take down the thickly woven baskets and wicker colanders
for wine;
with fresh well water mix in that offending earth
and pack it to the brim; as you'd expect, the moisture
dribbles through in heavy drops.
The tip of the tongue of anyone who takes on to try it

will tell the tale, his turned-up mouth squirming with the taste.
And so, in short, a richer soil is tested, too—
toss it from hand to hand and it won't crack or crumble,
250 no, it clings to fingers just like pitch.

    Soggy soil gives massive growth, more than's natural.
Preserve me from such profusions,
or such excess when new shoots show!
Whether soil is light or heavy you'll know without a word.
A glance will tell black earth, or whatever colour
it turns out to be. It's harder far to figure out
earth that's cursed to be cold, though now and then giant pines,
poisonous yews, and dark climbs of ivy give a clue.

    Keep all this in mind. Let moisture burn off from the ground,
260 divide the uplands into trenches,
turn over any clods of earth to face winds from the north—
all this before you set your sprigs of vine. A crumbly soil
is best of all—broken down by grace of frosts and freezing
    winds,
and the ongoing toil of diggers who have worked the plot, perch
    by perch and rood by rood.

    But those whose eyes watch everything miss nothing.
Begin by searching out two soils that are the same in which to
    start your seedlings
in order that when, by and by, you transplant them
they won't feel any difference from what surrounds their mother
    tree.
What's more—you print the mark of compass points onto the
    bark
270 to show which way each used to face and know which bore the
    heat
of southern suns, which kept its back hunched to the north,
so deep ingrained are habits formed in younger days.

    Ask yourself, before you start, whether it's best to place your
    vines
on rising ground, or flat. If it's a fertile plain you plan to set
lay out your plants together. Close sowing won't put brakes on
    Bacchus.

But if it's land that rises up to touch the sky, or hills that reach
    into the distance,
be generous with room between the rows. Make sure that they
    run parallel
and still maintain right angles* with the boundary lines,
the way in war you'd often see a legion massed in ranks,
its cohorts standing—and standing out—on open ground,   280
aligned and at the ready, the everywhere just like a glittering
    stretch of sea,
and the flash of bronze, the clash of conflict still not started,
though the god of war roams edgily, in and out among battalions.
    Let all the avenues be equal,
not only so an idle eye might linger on the view
but because no other method gets the earth to give in matching
    measures
and grants the boughs free rein and the run of air.
    And you'll wonder maybe how far down to dig.
I'd be happy, I believe, to set the vines in shallow trenches.
But trees need to be driven deeper, and none more than   290
the dun must oak which holds its head to heaven,
with as much above the ground as its roots below delve into the
    pits of Tartarus.
And so it can't be overthrown by wintry weather, gusts of wind
or spills of rains, as it stands undaunted, outlasting lives
of sons and grandsons, a vanquisher of ages.
Far and wide it spreads its sturdy boughs, its branches hanging,
and in their midst its trunk, the mainstay of its massive shade.
    Whatever else you do, don't have your vineyard face toward
    the setting sun;
sow no hazels in the rows; don't pinch the main part
of the shoot, nor prune the topmost splays of trees—   300
they love the earth so tenderly—you mustn't brush against a
    sapling
even with blunt instruments; don't introduce wild olive stakes.
    For careless shepherds often cause a fire by letting fall a spark
that smoulders unobserved beneath the oily bark
and then runs riot among the leaves, racing

its rowdy roar as it chases sideways on and up,
lording it over every branch and the tips of every trunk,
enveloping the wood in flames and belching skywards clouds
of soot-filled smoke, the more so if a gale spins through
310 the forest roof and winds rush in to fan the blaze.

When the like of this occurs, plants give up the ghost.
Burn grafted trees to the roots, and they're left with nothing left
    to give,
nothing their own. Cut to the quick, they'll never send the same
    green shoots
out from deep below the ground. Oleaster that's all leaf and little
    fruit stands to triumph.

Pay no heed to anyone, however well he's versed in plant
    production,
who tells you to begin to plough rock-solid land while north
    winds still
bare their teeth. When winter seals the countryside
broadcast corn can't get a foothold in the soil.
It's spring's first flush that's best for sowing vines,
320 when that bright bird returns, the bane of lanky snakes,
or, if not then, the first cold snap of autumn, before the sun's
fiery steeds have touched on winter, although, in truth, the
    summer's gone already.

Spring it is, spring that's good to the core of the wood, to the
    leaves of groves,
spring that reawakens soil and coaxes seeds to fruitfulness.
It's then almighty father, Air, marries the earth*
and penetrates her with prolific showers, and, their bodies joined
as one, unbridles life's potential.

The woodlands off the beaten track reverberate with singing
    birds
and, right on time, cattle come into their season—
330 the countryside stands to deliver—and in the warmth of western
    breezes
the plains let down their very breasts; a gentle wash infuses
    everything
and new growth ventures to believe it's safe beneath the young,

still unfamiliar sun, and vine shoots fear no southern gales
nor roaring northerlies that scour rain clouds from the sky;
rather, they prompt their buds to boldness and leaves to colour
everywhere. That days were not that different at the dawning
of the world I can easily believe, nor proceeded differently.
Then it was spring, all basked in spring,
and winter's winds bit their tongue—
all this when livestock first unclosed their eyes   340
and man, begot of rocks, first held up his head,
with creatures loosed to roam woodscape and stars to ramble
     skies.
   Indeed, how could such tender growth survive vicissitudes
if there were not between the cold and warmth a spell of
     dreamlike quiet,
when heaven's kindness brought its gift of ease?
What's more, whenever you set down your slips
don't forget to land them well,
or dig in around them bits of pervious stone and broken shells.
It's known well that waters will soak through them
and their gentle vapours spread to pick the plants' spirits up.   350
Men have experimented by laying slabs and broken tiles
to offer them protection from the pouring rain or, even, on those
     days
the Dog Star's heat intensifies to parch and crack the soil.
   When you've your seedlings put to bed you've still to go over
     the ground,
time and again, up to where the vine appears, scuffling soil
with your clawed hoe, to plough the earth steadily
and steer your straining oxen up and down the vineyard rows.
Then prepare the pliant reeds, whittled sticks and stakes of
     ash,
the sturdy forked supports through whose assistance
they can begin to climb fearless of wind   360
and fit themselves to the crowns of elms.
And all the while they're putting out their fragile leaves
treat the shoots with gentlest care, and while their branches
venture high, given free rein in the sky,

don't even glance against them with the pruning hook's keen
    edge—
no, use your fingertips to pluck this one here, and that one
    there.
And in due course, when they've their arms around those trees
(a strong embrace), it's time to trim their tops, time
to crop their branches (prior to this they'll wilt before any iron
    implement),
370 impose your will and curb their wayward leaders.
There are hedges to be laid, to keep out each and any beast,
especially when the leaves are delicate and unaccustomed to
    attack,
winter's cruelty or the worst extremes of summer,
not to mention rampant buffalo and deer nibbling havoc there,
or sheep and brawly heifers that eat their fill.
No winter weather, its hardest frosts,
nor summer's heat that splits the stones,
did hurt to them to equal herds and flocks,
their toothmarks' harm, the scars they've inscribed in the bark.
380   And they're the why, such transgressions, a goat is sacrificed
on every altar to the wine god—since our elders started to stage
    plays
and the sons of Theseus rewarded talent along the highways and
    the byways
and, with drink taken, took to hopping here and there,
a dance on greasy hides, and toppling in soft grass.
So, too, Ausonian settlers—who came from Troy—
recited their rough-hewn verse to entertain the masses,
and put on scary masks cut out of bark
and called on you, Bacchus, in rousing song,
and in your honour dangled from the tips of pines tender
    tokens.*
390 And it ensues that every vineyard crests and fills,
valleys teem, and deep ravines—
anywhere the god took in with his goodly gaze.
    Therefore, as is only right, we accord to Bacchus due respect
with songs our fathers sang and trays of baked offerings

and, led by the horn, the sacrificial puck is set before the altar
and his spewling innards roasted on hazel skewers.
　　Still there's more to do in the upkeep of the vines,
the work that's never finished, for every year, three times or
　　four,
you have to air the soil, by crushing clods time and time
　　again
with your hoe's heel, and not neglect to relieve the whole　　　400
　　plantation
of its load of leaves.
　　　　　　　　　　The farmer's chores come round
in seasons and cycles, as the earth each year retraces its own
　　tracks.
And even while the yard relinquishes the last, lingering
　　leaves
and a northerly divests woods of their panache
the keen countryman is turning thoughts to the year ahead
and all that's to be done in it: with his curved blade he'll prune
　　each branch
and shape it to his own design. Then, as soon as possible,
he'll rake the bed, set fire to his cuttings,
bring under cover vine supports and then, as late as late can be,
he'll draw the harvest home. Time and again, year on year,　　410
vines bow beneath a cloud and sink into the grip of
　　undergrowth—ever more to do!
So cast a hungry eye on a big estate if you're inclined,
but tend a small one.
　　　　　　　　　What's more, you'll find throughout the
　　woods rough sprigs
of butcher's broom and all along the river banks reeds needing to
　　be trimmed,
and, elsewhere, willows crying out for your attention—that will
　　keep you on the go.
Say grape branches are bound up, orchards finished with the
　　pruning hook,
and the vine-dresser furthest down the rows starts to sing of
　　work well done,

you've still to hoe the earth, to scuff and shuffle the light soil,
and keep a weather watch on the clusters as they ripen.

420 On the other hand, the olive thrives almost by neglect,
needing no encounter with hooked hoe or sickle blade
once it's found its feet in fields and faced the winds (and faced
    them down).
The earth itself, once it's been broken open, provides sufficient
    moisture
for growing plants to yield rich harvests in the ploughshare's
    wake.
That's the way you'll cultivate the best of olives—choice of
    Peace.
    Just as apples, as soon as they have sensed a surge of
      strength
along their trunks, stretch quickly for the stars all on their own—
they need no helping hand from us.
And all the while wild woodlands teem with fruits,
430 and the preserves of birds blaze with blood-red berries.
    Clover's cut for fodder. Deep woods provide pitch pines
that feed the evening fires and broadcast light.
Have men still second thoughts about setting seeds and the
    attendant cares?
What ties me to the theme of bigger trees? Broom and lowly
    willow
supply sufficient food for stock and shade for countrymen,
hedges for crop land and honey's essence.
What joy to feast my eyes on waves of boxwood by Cytorus
and on the stands of pine near Narycum,* what joy to set my
    sights
on fields no mattock ever scratched, that owe no debt to human
    effort.
440 Even in those fruitless forests found in the heights of
    Caucasus
which south-east winds assault and batter
each tree gives something of its own—the pines give timber,
    wood that's good

for building boats, the cypresses and cedars wood that's good for
    building houses.
And it's from here that countrymen procured turned spokes for
    wheels,
and axles for their waggons, and the long curved keels of their
    ships.
    No bother to the willow, a source of withies; nor to the elm, of
    foliage for fodder;
while myrtle shafts make sturdy spears, as do the cornel
    cherry's—
the best for war. Yews are best for the Ituraean bows.*
Soft lime and boxwood polished on a lathe
surrender to the shape the chisel's edge imposes;   450
while the alder, launched into its raging torrents, speeds
    sprightly
down the Po, and swarms of bees* set up their colonies
in hollow cork and the belly of a boast holm oak.
What offerings from Bacchus are more worthy of remembering?
Bacchus! He it was who gave cause to crime, he who smote
the maddened Centaurs* with a mortal blow—Rhoecus, Pholus,
and Hylaeus, the one who'd deranged the Lapiths with a power
    of wine.
    If they but knew! They're steeped in luck, country people,
being far removed from grinds of war, where earth that's just
showers them with all that they could ever ask for.   460
So what if he hasn't a mansion with gates designed to impress
and callers traipsing in and out all morning long.
So what if there's no rabble gawking at the entrance with its
    gaudy tortoiseshell veneer,
and tapestries with gold filigree, and bronzes plundered on a
    march to Corinth.
So what if their wool's merely bleached and not stained with
    Assyrian dyes,
and the olive oil they use hasn't been diluted with that tint of
    cinnamon—
no, what they have is the quiet life—carefree and no deceit—
and wealth untold—their ease among cornucopiae,

with grottoes, pools of running water and valleys cool even in
    warm weather,
470 the sounds of cattle and sweet snoozes in the shade.
There are glades and greenwoods, lairs of game,
young men wed to meagre fare but born and built for work.
Here, too, is reverence for god and holy fathers, and it was
    here
that Justice left her final footprints as she was taking leave of
    earth.
    And as for me, my most ardent wish is that sweet Poetry,
whose devotee I am, smitten as I've been with such commitment,
would open up to me the courses of the stars in heaven,
the myriad eclipses of the sun and phases of the moon,
whence come earthquakes, which are the reason deep seas surge
480 to burst their bounds before receding peacefully,
and are the why winter suns dash to dip themselves into the
    ocean
and are what causes long nights to last and linger.
But if I am not the one to sound the ways of the world
because my heart's lack of feeling stands in the way,
then let me be satisfied with rural beauty, streams bustling
    through the glens;
let me love woods and running water—though I'll have failed.
    Oh, for the open countryside
along the Spercheus, or the mountains of Taygetus,* its horde
    of Spartan maidens
ripe for the picking! Oh, for the one who'd lay me down to rest
in cool valleys of the Haemus range and mind me in the shade of
    mighty branches!
490   That man* has all the luck who can understand what makes
    the world
tick, who has crushed underfoot his fears about
what's laid out in store for him and stilled the roar of Hell's
    esurient river.
Indeed he's blessed, who's comfortable with country gods—
Pan and old Sylvanus,* and the sorority of nymphs.
High public office doesn't turn his head, nor regal pomp,

nor civil strife when friends and allies are at odds,

nor the Dacian league descending from the Danube,

nor even all concerns and cares of Rome, or any one provisional
domain.

For those with wants he feels a sorrow, not envy for the ones with
none.

The fruit on trees, all the country offers for the taking,   500

he'll gather. To cruel codes of law, or madding market places,

or the public record office—he simply gives no thought.

   Others rush in rowboats into uncharted waters, and race to
take up arms,

they work their way into the inner courts and chambers of the
king.

This man aspires to the sack of Rome itself, all its poor hearths
and homes,

just so he might imbibe from cups inlaid with gems and sleep
beneath the coverings of an emperor.

That man stockpiles a fortune while he broods on buried
treasure.

This man looks on with open mouth at speakers in the forum,
while that one is struck dumb

by the applause that punctuates the talk of senators and even
common people,

and ripples all the way along the benches, while others still spill   510
their brothers' blood

and ne'er a care. They strike out from the home place and forge
a life in exile,

searching for warm welcome in a fatherland* beneath a foreign
sun.

   A countryman cleaves earth with his crooked plough. Such is
the labour

of his life. So he sustains his native land and those who follow

in his footsteps; so he supports a team of oxen and keeps cattle
in good order.

All go and no let up—so that the seasons teem with fruit,

fields fill up with bullocks, and big arms of barley stand in
stooks.

They've overflowed the furrows, they'll burst the barns.
    Come winter, and the best of olives run spilling from the
        mills,
520 the pigs come back aglow on feeds of acorns, the arbutus tree
refreshes its pale foliage—and in such ways the autumn serves
        its bounty,
while up on open ground the vintage basks on boulders and
        ripens in the sun's caress.
    And all the while dear sons await each show of his affection,
his home remains a model of propriety, with milkers plunging
their four quarters, and kids delighting in lush pastures
and locking horns in playful jousts.
The countryman observes his holidays by taking ease out in the
        fields
with friends around a fire, garlands adorning goblets
from which they'll drink to you, Bacchus, as he arranges contests
        and competitions
530 for the hired help, hurling javelins at a target marked out on an
        elm,
and sturdy hands undress themselves for wrestling bouts.
    That was the life, and those the ways the Sabines cultivated in
        the days of old,
they, and Remus and his brother, so there could be no doubt
that Tuscany would go from strength to strength* and Rome
        become
gem of the world, embracing seven hills inside a single wall.
In days before a Cretan king held sway, times
when sacrilegious races fed on sacrificial oxen,
that was the life enjoyed on earth by splendid Saturn,*
when they were yet to hear the flare of battle trumpets
540 and the battering out of swords upon an anvil.
But we have covered vast tracts of matter and, besides,
it's high time that we released the sweating horses from their
        halters.

BOOK THREE

You too, Pales, great goddess of the folds, and you, Apollo, who
    tended flocks,
and all of you, woods and waters of Arcadia, we'll mind for ever
    in our songs.
They're tired themes that might have once engaged the lazy
    intellect
in Poetry—who hasn't heard of Eurystheus (who heaped
    hardships onto Hercules)
or of the altars established by Busiris which none could love?
Who hasn't told the tale of Hylas (and his boy's loss at sea), of
    Latona from the isle of Delos,
of Hippodamia and Pelops, that outstanding rider, his shoulder
    reconstructed out of ivory.*
What I need is to find a way I too can rise in triumph
from the earth and live on in the mouths of men.*
    I'll be the first, the very first, if I'm let live long enough,   10
to bring back to my own place from the heights of Helicon* the
    prize of the Muses—
I'll be the first to bring back to you, Mantua, the palms of
    Idumaea,*
and I'll erect a marble temple in a grassy meadow by the waters
of the wide Mincius whose ambling course flows this way and
    that,
its sides tossing their fringe of wavy rushes.
At its centre I'll place Caesar,* master of the shrine,
and in his honour—the day being mine—resplendent in my
    purple robes,
I'll drive five score of teams-of-four up and down along the bank.
    Because of me, all Greece will leave the Alpheus and the
        cypress groves of Molorchus*
to compete in running races and bruising bouts of boxing,   20
while I, presiding, my brow wreathed in a chaplet of clipped
    olive leaves,

administer the offerings. Already I can see how pleased I'll
        be
to front that rich procession and observe the sacrificial slaughter
        of young stock;
or, when the stage is set, to see it turn and open on a change of
        scene
as ornate curtains rise to reveal embroidered Britons in the
        backdrop.
On its doors I will have carved in gold and solid ivory
images of battle, of the Ganges, and the all-conquering
        regiments of Romulus,
and, yes, the mighty Nile in the full flood of war,
and columns springing up and decorated with bronze prows of
        battleships.
30 And I'll add in the Asian cities we've defeated and Niphates'
        heights we've overcome,
and the deceiving Parthian who feigns to turn his thought to
        flight
and—imagine—fires arrows backwards, and that pair of
        trophies snatched
from different enemies, those races twice defeated at two far
        edges of the ocean.*
    Then I'll set up, cut in stone from Paros, statues standing in
        relief so true to life
they seem to breathe, the scions of Assaracus,* famous race of
        Jupiter,
the founding father Tros, and he who set up Troy, Apollo;
Jealousy, from which no good could ever come, will quake and
        quiver before Cocytus,
that grim river, and Ixion tied to a rotating wheel with writhing
        snakes for ropes,
and the rock that bested everyone.*

40 Meanwhile we'll trace the Dryads' woods and virgin glades,
no little task that you've laid out for me, Maecenas,
for without encouragement from you, what could I amount to?
        Come on! Help me

shake off this lassitude. Mount Cithaeron is raucous with the
    roars of hunters,
Taygetus with the loud looing of hounds and Epidaurus,* home
    place of horse-handlers,
and, among the trees, the echoes ring, and what they're urging is
    Yes, yes.
   That time's not far away when I'll have girt myself to sing of
    Caesar's hard-fought battles
and guarantee he'll live, in name and fame, down all the years
that separate the first emergence of Tithonus* from his own
    appearance.

Whether it's in hope of taking gold at the Olympics a man keeps
    a string of horses,
or to have them fit to pull the plough he keeps strong bullocks,   50
he must, above all else, take in the make-up of the mare and
    mother cow;
cattle choice for breeding have a ferocious look, unsightly head
and thickset neck, and dewlap dangling all the way from jowl to
    heel,
their flanks as long as long can be, everything outsize,
down to their hooves; they've a shaggy heap of ears beneath
    horns
that are curved inward. And I don't mind markings like the
    stains of milk
and cattle that from time to time resist the yoke
and ruffle their heads with a look that's more the look of a
    bull
and, when they shuffle here or there, sweep away their tracks
    with one swish of their tails.
The years appropriate to have them covered by the bull and left 60
    to calve
begin after they're four and end before they're ten.
Their other years, they're neither fit to breed nor hale enough to
    haul the plough,
so, while they have youth to burn, turn loose the bulls to run
    with them;

don't hesitate to have them know the ways of love
and so produce your own replacements, one after the one before.

Poor creatures that we are, the best days of our lives
are first to fly; along come sickness, sorrows and the sores
of age; and what sweeps us away only a mortal tide.
Let there never be a time you wouldn't introduce changes to
          improve your stock,
70 nor times you wouldn't go so far as to supplant them; rather than
          regret
your losses later, anticipate them, and each year take your
          chances on new blood.
    Horses, too, must be subjected to a course of similar selection.
On whatever ones you plan to keep for breeding
bestow particular attention from the start.
See at once how well-bred members of the herd as foals in
          fields
step lighter than the others and yet land their feet so daintily.
And one, the first and foremost, will lead the way to brave a river
and the hazards of an unfamiliar bridge.
And he won't tremble at a hollow din. His is a long tapered neck
80 and graceful head, his body firm, back broad,
and shoulders showing off their muscle. Roans and chestnuts
are to be preferred, duns and greys to be avoided.
And there's more—at the clang of distant armour
he can't stand still, he's all ears, flanks aquiver,
as he struggles to contain his fiery breath in flaring nostrils.
His mane is thick and settles on his right side when it's shaken.
That horse is in such fine fettle his spine lies in a hollow between
          both sets of loins.
His hooves resound as they eat up the ground and spit it out
          again.
    Such was Cyllarus, the horse that Pollux brought on to the
          rein,*
90 as was that pair of horses tackled by the war god, Mars,
to a double-tree, and the team of great Achilles—all these
Greek poets put on record. Nimble Saturn, at his wife's arrival,*

threw a horse's mane across his neck and, as he fled,
set Mount Pelion shaking with a stallion's snort.

   Your chosen one, weakened with a fill of illness or the weight
      of years—
keep him shut up at home, suppressing any sympathy for the
      dishonour
of his age, for an old stud has no heat in his performance
and fails to rise to the task. Brought to the fray,
he's little more to offer than you'd fan in a fire of straws.
He'll get all het up for nothing; so, take particular notice of his   100
      character
and vigour, and also of his pedigree, the dam and sire,
and the way he deals with sorrows of defeat, and wears the glory
      of a win.

   You've seen—surely you've seen—how in a race, right from
      the off,
the chariots will gobble ground to take the lead,
and the charioteers, their hopes sky high and hearts in mouth,
lean forward as they ply their whips
and strain to give the horses their head, pushing them on.
The wheels are turning so quickly they burn.
Now up, now down, as if they're poised for take-off.
And no let up, and no let off, they're kicking up such a storm.   110
On their backs they feel the clammy breath of their pursuers.
They're so hungry for the laurels; winning means so much to
      them.

   It was Erichthonius who hatched the thought of harnessing
      four horses
to a chariot and standing up as it sped him along, a conqueror.
The Lapiths,* all the way from Pelion, bequeathed to us bits and
      bridles
and—riders astride—the lunging ring, and taught the cavalry
to hit the ground running, fully armed, and how to quicken their
      mount's pace.

To stand at stud, to satisfy as charger or track-horse takes equal
      effort:

the experts cast about for colts with a turn of speed or spring in
their step,
120 ignoring how often an older horse rebuffed the foe and drove
him to flight,
or even if it's claimed he came from Epirus or Mycenae
and could trace his bloodline the whole way back to Neptune's
stable.*
  With this in mind, they're all go as the time draws near, the
time for breeding,
and spare no end of trouble to flesh him out and fatten him up,
the stallion they've selected and settled on as kingpin of the line.
They gather fresh greenery and serve his fill of grain and water
so there's no chance that he's not up to the job he seems so keen
to do,
no chance the standard of the sire be mirrored in a scrawny foal.
  On the other hand, they mean to keep the mares lean,
130 and when they see first signs of coming into heat
they refuse them fodder and deny them drink.
And what they do is jizz them up by galloping
and tire them out in the sun when the barns are creaking with
the weight of provender, and scraps of chaff flap and flitter on
the breeze.
  This they do so no amount of indolence can curb their field of
fruitfulness
nor clog and leave its furrows void,
but, instead, so that love's seed be grasped and tucked away
deep where it should come to rest. Concern for sires dwindles
then and the care
for mares increases. Then, their months gone on and they're
now
140 full with foal, let no one hitch them to a heavy waggon,
nor let them take a running jump across a roadway,
or go racing through the grasslands or swimming in a river's
wrath.
They're best pastured in broad meadows alongside a brimming
stream,
a moss blanket all around and a bank of rich grazing,

shelter for protection and rock shadows stretching on the
  ground.
Around the caves of Silarus and the oaks that turn Alburnus so
  many shades of green
there swarms a pest, whose Latin name is *asilus*—
the horse- or warble-fly, but which the Greeks call *oestrus*,
that is frenzy, whose maddening hum is the bane of whole herds
and sends them scurrying from woods, the air itself in shock,   150
a rage of roars and bellows, as is the Tanager's dried-up river
  bed.
This is the pest that Juno conjured once, that time, her ire
  incensed,
she turned into a heifer Io, daughter of Inachus.*
And so, because the midday's heat intensifies its threat,
you must safeguard the cows in calf and let the cattle out
only when sun's starting up or nightfall's ushering in the stars.
  Once they've been delivered, the farmer's focus switches to
    the scions.
He'll stint no time in reckoning them as members of the herd,
or branding those he'll hold on to for breeding,
or those he'll designate for sacrificial ceremonies   160
and those with which he'll cleave the ground and roll rough sods.
All that's left, he'll dismiss to graze in pastures of green plenty.
But those he'll school to shape for service of the land
he'll break and bring on while still calves,
an agile age, still young and innocent.

So, to begin—loop rings of wicker loosely round their necks;
then, when those once unrestricted begin to bend to your will,
and still fitted with that same collar,
yoke them in matching pairs and make them march in step.
Time and time again, let them drag an empty waggon,   170
one so light it leaves hardly a track or trace in dust.
In due time, an axle made of beech, well worn and glistening,
may creak beneath its heavy weight, the wheels fixed to a beam
    finished with bronze ferrules.
  And all the while, as they go on, in their wild ways,

for them you'll gather, as well as hay and sedge and spindly strips
    of willow leaves,
corn you've cropped by hand. Don't, the way they used to do
when cows produced, work them to fill the churns with creamy
    milk—no,
save all that flows from their spins to feed the young they're
    doting on.

But, if you're more inclined toward the fare of war with
    troops
180 of fearless cavalry, or to have a team glide along the side of the
    river Alpheus,
site of games, and race around Jupiter's wild olive groves,
the first trial for a horse is to tolerate the clash of arms
and clamour of a conflict, not to shy from screeching wheels,
nor smart at jangling harness as he's standing in his stall—
that done, he should be more and more at home with his master's
    friendly tones
and grow to love the feeling of his neck being patted.
Accustom him to these when he's but barely off the teat
and still unsteady on his feet; next, fit him with a light bit and
    bridle
before he gets cute in his ways. Three years on, and coming into
190 his fourth summer, take him to the training ring
where he'll step out in equal paces,
his legs will fall and rise in a rotating motion,
and him the very picture of work.
                        Then he'll take on to race
the wind and fly across open spaces
(as if he's been given his full head),
leaving only faintest hoof-prints in the dirt
like one of those northerlies rushing from the Arctic
and suddenly dispersing crisp clouds in its way;
fields of corn and water stretches shiver in its path,
200 woodlands echo, and tides come crashing to the shore—
that's the wave that wind advances as it spends itself above the
    land and sea.

A horse the like of that either will work up a lather of sweat
    around the laps of Elis,
blood foaming from the bit, to pass the post in first position,
or be good for pulling Belgian chariots of war,* his neck
    responsive to the lightest touch on the reins.
Then and only then, when he's been broken, feed him his fill
of grain and green vetches to fatten him—for, until you have
    them eating out of the palm of your hand,
such stuff will make their spirits soar and they'll not be held in
    check,
they'll pay no heed to springy whip, no curb chain will restrain
    them.
In fact, there's nothing better to buttress your efforts to build up
    their strength
than to restrain them from love's drive and passion's   210
    undiscerning force.
And this is all the same, whether you're more interested in cattle
    or in horses.

You see, that's why they banish bulls to the back of beyond, to
    languish on their own
behind a mountain or the far side of a river's current,
or keep them locked in in pens well stocked with fodder.
For it's a fact, a female saps their strength and leaves them
    wasted by the sight of her
and turns their heads from thoughts of woodland fare and
    pasture,
so enchanting are her charms. She'll go so far as force
    contending rivals
to sort it out among themselves, and often by the wield of
    horns.
See her browsing in the mighty woods of Sila,* that handsome
    heifer.
See them locked in battle taking turns to deal a deadly blow,   220
now one, and now the other, their bodies red with blood,
one set of horns forward, one resisting, and it's all moans and
    groans

that echo round the forests the length and breadth of
      heaven.
    Fighting bulls won't want to share a stall—
the one, defeated, disappears, an outcast,
with sighs all round both for the wounds and the disgrace
      inflicted by
his vanquisher, and—indeed—for all he's lost, those unrequited
      loves.
And so, with one last look, he takes leave of his ancestral realm
and then begins to work out hard, with unrelenting exercise,
230 and beds down for the night on rock
with only thorny leaves and pointy sedge to eat.
Pushing, pushing himself, channelling rage into his horns
by charging trees, so he assails the air,
preparing for the fray by pawing ground and scattering the
      clods.
    Then, his strength recovered, powers restored,
responding to some secret sign he'll rush head first at his
      oblivious enemy
the way a wave begins to foam and froth at sea
and summons from the deep its lengthy curve and then,
      tumbling
towards the shore, makes a fearsome racket on the rocks, and
      breaks,
240 folding over like a mountain while the waves beneath it
whirl in eddies, disgorging from the ocean floor night-dark and
      dismal shingle.
    Man and beast, each and every race of earth,
creatures of the sea, domesticated animals, and birds in all their
      finery,
all of them rush headlong into its raging fury: love's the same for
      one and all.
No other time a lion cub could slip from his mother's mind
than when she roams the plains all hot and bothered, nor has the
      bear, the hideous,
ever wrought in woods such disorder and destruction.
Then, too, the wild boar's at its wildest, the tiger at her worst.

Oh no, that's not the time to go wandering on your own in the
    wilderness of Africa.*

See if every stallion doesn't shake and shiver in each pore   250
if a whiff of that familiar scent drifts down the wind and reaches
    him.

Nothing now keeps them in hand, not the rider's rein nor anger's
    whip;
not cliffs or rocky caves; nor sweeps of water act as obstacles
though they may snap at mountains and snatch them away in
    swirling surf.

    The Sabellian boar goes lumbering by, honing his tusks,
his trotters tearing up the ground, and grinding sides against a
    tree,
up and down, this way and that, until he has inured his flanks
    against injuries.

Spare a thought for that young man, his passion's fervour
    burning
to the quick. Needless to say, he swims a raging sea
late at night, not knowing where he's going, and all the while   260
    above his head
heaven's gate thunders and the rocky hazards reverberate in
    turbulence.

Nor can the cries of his demented parents bring him back,
nor the girl who'll waste away for want of him, and die of
    grief.

    Think of Bacchus' dappled lynxes, raging routs of wolves and
    curs,
and the way the placid stag reverts to battle in the rut,
and then forget them—the ferocity of mares consigns them to
    the shade.

What possessed them, only Venus, the day his own team turned
    on him
at Potniae and gobbled Glaucus, limb by limb?
There's nothing that can snaffle them when they're in season.
    Gargarus?

No. Nor roaring Ascanius. They'll make little of mountains,   270
    they'll straddle wide waters.

The minute the embers of their lusts flick into flame
(in spring, especially, when it's likeliest that they'll come into
    heat)
they'll turn, as one, towards the west to face the wind
and breathe its airs and then—a miracle!—without being
    covered
by a sire, receive the seed a breeze implants in them.
Then over rugged rock and bluffs and onto lower plains
they break into a gallop, not east to where day begins
but away, in all directions, north, north-west,
and where the southerlies cloud the sky with driving rain.
280   Then, and only then, a viscous fluid, which herdsmen have
    good cause
to call 'mare madness',* oozes out of their vaginas,
a mucus hags crave to collect to mix with herbs and hexes
and so concoct their wicked potions.

Time's flying by, time we'll never know again,
while we in our delighted state savoured our subject bit by bit.
Enough of herds of cows and horses—the last half of my task
    remains:
my report of sheep and goats, woolly ewes and straggly nannies.
Now you've your work cut out for you—stake your hopes of
    fame on it, courageous countrymen.
Don't think I'm not aware how hard it is to find the words
290 for such a theme and dignify one that's so circumscribed.
But love's sweet force transports me to Parnassian peaks
where none has ever trod before, where there's no beaten path
easing downward to the spring at Castalia.*
Now I appeal to you, Pales, inspire me with some authority.

First and foremost, I recommend you feed your sheep in
    comfort under roofs
until, in its due course, summer sings again, all leaves,
and spread armfuls of straw and ferns beneath them
so neither chills nor colds afflict your tender care
and bring on scab or foot rot—horrors you can't bear to see.

Moving on, I know the nanny needs a full supply of arbutus   300
and other bushes still in leaf, full access to free-flowing streams,
and a stall whose back abuts the wind but which can take
        advantage
of sun's highest heat in winter time, when cold Aquarius is
        waning
and sprinkles dew on a departing year.
If we tend these as carefully as sheep
equal good will come of them (despite the high prices
Milesian wool dyed with Tyrian reds will fetch).
For they give a greater yield, of both young and milk—however
        full
froth fills your pail, once you've stripped their udders
you'll find another flow if you pull on their spins again.   310

And that's not all—some shave the smigs off their grizzly
        chins
and shear the bristling hair off bucks from Cinyps*
for use by troops and as loose coverlets for sad and sorry men at
        sea.
They're kept to browse the woods and hills of Arcadia,
thorns and prickly brambles that thrive on higher grounds,
and—no need to call them—come back themselves, their kids in
        tow,
struggling to drag bags of milk across the threshold of the
        parlour.
So spare no efforts to shield them from the bite of frosts and icy
        winds—
they need so little minding in exchange for all they give;
leave mangers brimming over with hay and roughage   320
and them in reach of what's stored in the loft all winter long.

But when the west wind's gentle breezes summon them,
the sheep and goats, to summer in the outfields,
we'll make our way at crack of dawn and take to chilly
        pastures—
the day still young and grass a frosty glisten—
while dew the cattle love still lingers on fresh shoots.
Then, when the risen sun has honed a thirst

and crickets stir the plantings with their brittle song,
I'll bring the flocks to springs and standing pools
330 and let them drink from hardwood troughs.
But by high noon I'll have them forage for and find
a shady glen where one of those ages-old,
great girthed oaks of Jupiter stretches out stout branches
or a thickly planted holly grove lours in its own hallowed
shadows.
I'll have them drink again cool runs of water and browse
again
until the setting sun when twilight starts to chill the air,
its dews refresh the grazing, and cries of birds ring out again—
kingfishers from the shoreline, wood-warblers from the woody
groves.

You know those Libyan shepherds? Should I go on about them
in my verses—
340 their grazing-grounds and huts in settlements scattered here and
everywhere?
Many's the time they've spent the whole long day, and all night
too, for weeks on end,
tending flocks, out under stars, month after month,
and no sight or sign of anybody's house, so expansive is the
desert.
The African herd brings with him all he owns, hearth and home,
his weaponry, a hound from Amyclae, a quiver from Crete.
Much the same as any Roman brave, armed in his country's
cause,
advances bent beneath the burden of his kit and, still, before you
know it,
there he is, his camp already pitched, his enemy surprised.*
Not like these the tribes of Scythia and the Sea of Azor
350 where the Hister runs turbid with ochrous sands
and the Rhodope range reaches back to the central pole.*
They keep their cattle enclosed in stalls up there,
where there's neither a grass blade to be seen nor on the trees a
single leaf.

Instead, the ground goes on as far as far as eyes can see
and land looks all the same under mounds of snow and ice that's
    more than four men deep.
  Every day's a winter day, with hordes of north-west winds
    marauding.
And never once can Sun sneak through that washy desolation—
not when he rides to reach the heights of heaven, no,
nor when his team draws him to dip into the reddening brine.
And suddenly, in running rivers, the water grows a skin of bone. 360
The wave can bear wheels rimmed with iron;
what once was home to sterns of ships plays host to
    broad-beamed waggons.
Bronze vessels smash in smithereens, clothes harden on your
    back,
wine that flowed before is hacked with axes,
whole lakes transform to solid ice,
while icicles make unkempt beards hard as a board.
Meanwhile the snow continues falling.
Cattle catch their death of cold, ox hulks stand crouched
beneath a crust of frost; stags huddle numb beneath a bulk
the like of which they've never known, their antlers barely   370
    visible.
You don't need hounds to hunt them down, no, nor nets,
nor violaceous tassels for 'scares' to start them to stampede—
for as their breasts strain in vain against the massive piles
men simply slay them with the knives they have to hand and cut
    them up
to solemn sounds of sacrifice, and bear them off with shouts of
    celebration.
  As for those men, they carry on at ease in caves
they've gouged out underground, with stacks of hardwood by
    the hearth,
whole elms, in fact, to roll on to the roaring flame.
The nights they pass by playing games—quite satisfied with
    brew they've made
of bitter berries of the rowan ash, their substitute for draughts of 380
    wine.

For that's the kind they've always been, barbaric tribes north of
    here, born and reared
beneath the Big Dipper; at the mercy of the worst those east
    winds have to offer,
they bundle up in dusky cattle hides and pelts of wild animals.

If a crop of wool be your concern, nip them in the bud,
those burrs and thistles; steer clear of pastures in too good a
    heart
and, from the start, select a flock with spotless fleeces.
As for the ram, however white his wool, if he has as much
as one black spot beneath the crown of his moist mouth,
cast him aside—that speck will smudge the pureness of his
    progeny.
390 You'll find another soon enough; there's a world of them to
    choose from.
And so it was, if truth were told, that Pan of Arcadia wooed you,
the Moon.* By such immaculate designs he drew you to
the secret places of the wood, and you did not resist his call.

    But if it's milk you're after, hand pick and put before the herd
    in pens
plenty of lucerne, and clover, and salted grass,
for the minerals will whet their thirst and swell their elders
and flavour what they yield with a briny taste.
(There are those who wean the kids at birth by muzzling them
    with iron spikes.)
The milk you strip by dawn- or daylight you'll curdle in the
    night
400 and what you draw at dusk or dark
you'll cart away in wickerwork
when the shepherd goes to town
or sprinkle with a pinch of salt and set aside for winter use.
    Nor let the care of dogs be the last thing on your mind,
but feed them up as one on fattening whey, fleet-footed Spartan
    puppies
and a fierce Molossian mastiff: with them as watchdogs you'll
    need never fear

rustlers in your stalls at night, nor an attack of wolves,
nor Spanish thieves stealing up behind you.
And, as well, you'll put to flight wild asses that are easily scared
and course for hares and run down deer.   410
Often, too, your baying pack will oust wild boars from wallows in
    the woods
or, with the yelps of whelps across high ground,
you'll press a trophy stag into the nets you've set up there to trap
    him.
   Back in the stalls, learn to burn juniper that makes sweet-
    smelling smoke
and with the fumes of allheal's bitter resin evict any vile
    serpents.
Often underneath a disused shed you'll find a viper lurking, one
you wouldn't want to touch, that stole refuge from the light of
    day,
or else some other fanged creature, which takes to sneaking into
    the shed's protection,
is snuggling there, quite at home, the scourge of cattle.
Good shepherd, grab a rock, pick up a thick stick quickly   420
and, as he primes himself to threaten you, his cheeks puffed out,
finish him off. See, he's fled already and hidden in a hole.
From head to tail his winding coils unreel
until his final writhing stops.
   Then there is, deep in the gorges of Calabria, that ill-fated
    serpent,
with its protruding chest and coiling scaly back,
its lengthy belly blotched with distinctive markings,
and, as long as there are rivers gushing from their sources,
as long as earth is drenched by dews of spring and southern rain,
river banks are its abode, stagnant pools its dismal haunt,   430
and there it gluts its greedy gullet with fish and burping frogs.
But when those marshy lands dry up and sunshine splits the
    earth
it takes to solid ground, its blood-red eyes ablaze,
and with its savage thirst, made mad with heat, rampages
    through the countryside.

Oh, let me never contemplate a nap in open air
nor, in a grove up on a ridge, think of lounging on the grass
the moment he, his skin just sloughed, in flush of youth, slithers
     past,
his seed and breed left behind him, hatched or still inside the
     shell,
and preens himself before the sun and flicks and flashes in his
     mouth his three-forked tongue.*

440 I'll tell you, too, about diseases, their source and symptoms.
You'll have a flock tormented by the frantic itch of scab, when
     perishing showers
hit and run and midwinter's cruellest frosts cut them to the
     quick,
sweat clots and clings just above the britch wool
and jagged briars prick their flesh.
That's why the worthy shepherd dips his stock into fresh
     water—
and plunges rams into the flow to soak the fleece,
where they, let go, go sailing down the river.
Or else he'll rub bitter dregs of olive oil onto the newly shorn
and concoct a potion out of litharge, that is 'silver slag',
     mixing it
450 with steaming native sulphur, and pine-pitch from Mount Ida,
     with greasy wax
and squills, that is 'sea onions', and noxious hellebore and pitch-
     black bitumen.
You'll find no quicker cure, however, than if you brace yourself
to take a knife to lance an open sore,
for it's a fact infections thrive best undetected,
while a dithering herd hesitates to put his helping hand onto the
     wound
and instead sits idly by, imploring gods for better fortune.
    What's more, when pain pierces to the marrow those that
     bleat,
and rages there, a parching fever gnawing on their limbs,
you'll do well to cut into a vein at the bottom of their feet,

one that throbs with blood, to steer away the scalding heat,   460
as was the custom with the Bisaltae and fierce Gelonians
when they roved around the mountain ranges and the outposts
    of the Getes
and drank a mix of clotted milk and horse's blood.
   Then, if you happen to catch sight of a ewe that's seeking
    refuge
in a far-off shade or picking listlessly at just the tips of grass,
that dilly-dallies way behind the others, or is lying slump down
in the middle of the field, or at night slinks off all on her own,
waste no time in exscinding that malignance with your blade
before the dread disease creeps through your whole unwitting
    flock.
   They're no more plentiful, nor furious, those squalls that   470
    strike from out at sea,
than the onset of these plagues*—it's not one here, another
    there,
death smites, but all in one fell swoop, the fill of outfields,
what is now and what's to come, the hope of herds, root and
    branch and blossom.
So let him learn by looking, who casts his eye from the apex of
    the Alps
to the ramparts of Noricum and the plains by the Timavus,
how after all that fell the shepherd's realm is now deserted,
and the grazing grounds left to waste, the length and breadth of
    them.
For here it was that once, with its seed in disease that wafted on
    the wind,
a time of misery took hold and festered in the sweat of autumn
to decimate all kinds of animals, including savage ones;   480
it contaminated drinking water and spoiled the foodstore with a
    blight.
Nor was the road to death straightforward: rather,
when thirsts had parched every vein and made each joint shrivel
    up in agony,
there was a second flood of fluids which caused the very bones
to crumble, as bit by bit this cancer did them in.

Indeed, there have been times, mid-ceremony, that the victim
    of the offering
standing by an altar, as the snow-white woolly bandeau was
    being wreathed
around its head, dropped dead before the acolytes could act,
or when the priest had struck the sacrificial blow
490 the entrails laid out on the altar failed to flare into flame
and the best of prophets were defeated in attempts to read
and to unravel what's to come. Stick a knife beneath the skin and
    the blade's
hardly marked; what trickles out barely leaves a blemish in the
    dirt.
There are calves dropping in droves in the middle of rich
    pastures,
giving up the ghost in sight of hay-filled mangers.
House-trained dogs go raving mad; a fit of coughing
racks the pigs, blocks their swollen windpipes and leaves them
    bereft of breath.
Even that horse, a champion once, falls victim to ill-fortune,
and, off both his food and drink, totters as he stamps the floor,
500 his ears fall forward and a fitful sweat surrounds them,
the one that signifies the final onslaught.
Hard to the touch, his coat you pat, and there's no give in it.
    Such are the signs in the early days of being at death's door—
but if disease proceeds to tighten its grip,
then, yes, the eyes begin to flicker, laboured breath
is interspersed with moans and groans, a rattle
shudders from the groin, blackened blood oozes from the
    nostrils,
clogged passages close in around an arid tongue.
Some deemed it a help to drench them with a winey liquid
    poured through a horn,
510 one chance to make the dying well. But soon this too proved
    useless:
they were restored just long enough for fevers to flare up again,
and though they were already under a mortal pall (forfend
    that we

have such a fate, we who stayed true to you; send such ends to
    our enemies),
with their bare teeth they tore their own frayed limbs to
    shreds.
   Behold a bull, all hot and heavy, his shoulder to the plough,
how he collapses, drooling blood and foam and froth, and with a
    moan
heaves his last. The ploughman goes with heavy heart
to untack his mourning mate, then simply walks away
and leaves his plough plonk in the middle of the field.
Not tall trees' shade, nor the pleasures of sweet meadows   520
proffer consolation, no, nor that river scampering over rocks,
more pure than amber, as it makes its way towards the plain.
His flanks cave in, a glazed look overcasts his eyes,
and his neck's a stone as it inclines towards the earth beneath the
    burden of itself.
   All the work he did, all he contributed—and to what end?
    What came of it,
his turning of the heavy acres? His like was never once in thrall
    to wines
transported from Campania, nor did they ever do
damage to themselves by indulgence, feast after feast.
For them a simple diet of leaves and plain grass, their drink clear
    springs
and running streams; nothing disturbs their sleep, they've no   530
    worries in the world.
   There was talk that was the only time
you'd be hard-pressed to find cattle fit for the ritual to Juno,
when to the temple front they led mismatched pairs of oxen they
    hadn't even broken.
No wonder they would scrabble in the ground with mattocks
and cut their fingers to the bone planting saplings
and strain to drag creaking carts up hill, down dale, and their
    own necks shouldering the yoke.
Wolves no longer lurk in ambush near the folds
nor prowl at night around the flock—more pressing cares
have made them tame. You'll find shy does and timid hinds

540 straggling in and out among the hounds and in between the
          houses.
     Now all the creatures of the deep, indeed everything that
          swims,
     lie washed up on the farthest shore as if they were the victims of
          a shipwreck,
     and seals escape upriver where they have never been before,
     the viper meets its end failing to defend its labyrinthine hiding
          place,
     as do watersnakes, caught off guard, their scales bristling.
     The air itself is no fit place for birds; down they plunge
     and forfeit life somewhere among the clouds above.
     What's more, a change of pasture altered nothing.
     What cures they looked for caused but harm, and they gave up;
550 who were to know it all knew nothing: Chiron, son of Phillyra;
          Melampus, son of Amythaon.*
     Unleashed, a pale-faced fury came rampaging—Tisiphone—
     an emissary into light out of hell's darkness, sowing seeds of
          distress and disease,
     and every day, bit by bit, she held her hungry head up higher.
     With the bleating of sheep and loud roars of cattle
     the dried-up rivers rang, those and the rolling hills.
     Then she caused them to die in droves, and rotting carcasses,
     smitten by the epidemic, piled up—even in the pens—
     until men learned to open pits and lay them covered
          underground.
     Their hides were useless now—you couldn't find the water that
          would wash
560 those corpses, nor flame or fire that would do away with them.
     You couldn't even save the wool, the sores had so corrupted
          fleeces
     you couldn't let them near your loom.
     In fact, if anyone tried on a garment made from them
     he'd break out in a fester of pustules
     and foul-smelling sweat. Not long now before
     that rank contagion would begin to gnaw on cursèd limbs.

BOOK FOUR

Which brings me to heaven's gift of honey,* or manna, if you
    will.
Lend kind ears to this part, my lord, Maecenas, in which
    I'll tell
about a small society comprising systems worthy of your high
    esteem.
Its leaders great of heart, its customs, character, and conflicts—
these I'll report, bit by bit, as is appropriate.
A humble theme—but far from humble is the fame
for one spared by the gods, if his voice attract Apollo's ear.

First find a site and station for the bees
far from the ways of the wind (for wind obstructs them bringing
    home
whatever they may forage), with neither ewes nearby nor butting 10
    kids
to trample down the blossom—to say nothing of a heifer
straying through the dew and flattening growing grass.
And keep out from their grazing grounds the lizard with its
    ornate back,
the bee-eater, and other creatures of the air,
not least the fabled swallow, Procne, her breast still bearing
    stains* from her bloodied hands,
for all of these lay widespread waste—they'll snatch your bees
    on the wing
and bear them off in their mouths, a tasty snack for greedy
    nestlings.
  Make sure you have at hand clear springs and pools with
    moss-fringed rims,
a rippling stream that rambles through the grass,
and have a palm or outsize oleaster to cast its shadow on the 20
    porch,
so that, in spring that they so love, when sent out by the queens

first swarms of young and new bees issued from the hive
may play; a river bank nearby might tempt them to retire from
    the heat
and, on their way and in their way, a leafy tree entices them to
    tarry.
Whether water there is standing still or flowing
lob rocks into its middle and willow logs to lie crosswise
so they'll have stepping stones where they can take a rest
and spread their wings to dry by the fires of the sun, all this
in case an east wind occurred to sprinkle them
30 while they were dawdling, or dunked them head first in the
    drink.
Let all around be gay with evergreen cassia, spreads of fragrant
    thyme
and masses of aromatic savory. Let violet beds absorb moisture
    from the rills and runnels.

So to the hives themselves. Whether you've woven them of
    hollowed bark
or laid down a thatch of supple twigs,
give them a narrow opening. For winter's cold
makes honey hard, just as surfeit of heat causes it to melt and
    run.
Fear each of these extremes in equal measure. It's not for
    nothing
bees seal their tiny ceiling vents with daubs of wax,
or close the openings with a mastic made from flower blossoms.
40 And to this very end they generate accumulations of such glue,
more viscous than birdlime or pitch from Asia Minor.
And frequently, they'll even dig a hiding place (if what is told is
    true)
to make a snug home underground; or be discovered
ensconced within the cavities of pumice and the chambers of
    dead trees.
But you, you should still skim their leaky nests with light coats of
    mud
to keep them warm, and top them with a layer of leaves.

And don't allow a yew tree grow near their abode;
don't roast red crabs at your hearth, don't risk a murky pool,
nor anywhere where there's a pungent odour, nor any place
where hollow rocks return with eerie echoes anything you say.   50
  And furthermore, when the golden sun has beaten winter
    back
below the ground and aired the sky in summer's light,
they lose no time in touring woods and fields and sampling fruits
    of flowers
and sipping from the water's brim—and all this while they're on
    the wing;
and, though enraptured by such strange delight,* they mind
their nestlings and newborn, seed and breed of them,
and use their special skills to shape new cells and press the sticky
    honey home.
Then, when you lift your eyes and see a swarm discharged
to ride the skies, a moving smudge through summer,
and marvel at a darksome cloud trailing down the wind,   60
keep note of how they make—yes—make a beeline
for fresh water and a leafy shade. Then, in that very spot,
sprinkle tastes prescribed as treats: balm you've crushed,
blades of honeywort and borage; have Cybele's cymbals fill the
    air.
They'll make themselves at home in this charmed site,
and set up on their own—as is their wont—a cradle for their
    young in its inner reaches.
  On the other hand, if maybe they've come out for fight—for
    frequently,
when you've two queens,* troubles explode in all-out civil war,
as quick as lightning you'll pick up on the common mood and
    feel
from miles away a restiveness, raring to go, hearts set on   70
    confrontation.
There you'll hear martial music—a raucous theme to galvanize
    the undecided,
a swarming tone that brings to mind the broken blasts of a bugle-
    horn.

Then, though they're agitated, they assemble; their pinions
    gleam and glint,
and on their beaks they hone their stings; they are limbering up.
They jostle round the queen, the whole way to her headquarters,
and with loud noises challenge their enemies to engage.
Then, on a given day—clear skies, fields plain to see—
they'll burst out of the entranceway, charge, lock forces high in
    the sky—
a mounting racket—and, mingled and massed into a ball,
80 trip and fall headlong: never was hail thicker,
nor a shower of acorns that rained down from a shaken oak.

    The queens themselves proceed along the ranks, their wings
        conspicuous,
a mighty passion seething in their tiny frames,
determined not to give an inch until the victor's heavier hand
has forced one side or other to turn their backs and run.
And still a rising so incensed, or combat so enormous,
a mere handful of dust will check and put to rest.

    But when you have recalled both leaders from the battle
select the one that looks the worse for wear and do him down, to
    death,
90 to save all that would be a waste on him and leave the way open
    for his vanquisher
to hold sway in the hive.

                    For you'll find there are two kinds of
    bees—
the one aglow with golden flecks—the one you want—
its bright, distinguished reddish mail; the other a sight,
the picture of pure laziness, its sagging paunch distended to the
    ground.
And as there are two sets of qualities in queens, so the masses
differ too, one sort a dread, just like that traveller who fetches up
caked in dust and spits out dirt to clear his throat;
the other resplendent, their brightness flashing,
with matching specks of gold a pattern on their bodies.
100 It's their offspring you'd favour: from them, at the appointed
    time,

you'll get the best of honey, not just the best for sweetness,
but for clearness, too, and its ability to take the edge off a rough
    wine.
  But when the swarms fly off without a point or purpose and
    caper
in the sky with no thought for their combs and leave their homes
    to cool
you must intervene to sway their idle minds from such
    inconstant play;
nor is that intervention hard: pick up the queens, pinch their
    wings and pluck them off.
While they stay put, none of the others dares take to the air,
nor budge a standard from the camp.

Let there be gardens to amuse them, with the scent of brightly
    coloured flowers.
Let Priapus of Hellespont* stand guard,   110
armed with a curved willow branch to fend off attacks by birds
    and burglars.
Have him, and none but him, who cares to do such things, carry
from the mountains thyme and wild laurel, and set them all
    around the hives;
have him, and none but him, wear his hands hard with work;
have him, and none but him, plant healthy plants and water
    them with friendly showers.

Indeed, if I were not already near the limit of my undertaking,
furling my sails and hurrying my prow to shore,
it may be that my song would turn to fruitful gardens and the
    loving labours
that embellish them, to those rose beds that flower twice a year at
    Paestum,
to how endive delights in drinking from the brook   120
whose banks are rife with celery, and how cucumber winds its
    way
through grass and swells into big bladders; nor would I not speak
    of

the narcissus, late to leaf, nor of the bendy stem of bear's breech,
    that is acanthus,
or pale ivy, or myrtle that's so fond of shores.
    I mind it well, beneath the arched turrets of Tarentum,
where deep Galaesus irrigates the goldening fields,
I set my eyes on an old man, a Cilician who
had a few forsaken roods that wouldn't feed a calf,
not to mention fatten cattle, and no way fit for vines.
130 Still, he scattered in the thickset his vegetables and a lily
    border,
vervain and poppies that you'd eat—in his mind the match of
    anything
a king might have, and when he came home late at night
he'd pile the table high with feasts no one had paid money for.
    In spring, with roses first for picking, and autumn, apples—
and yet, while winter's hardest frosts were splitting
stones in two and putting stops to water's gallop,
he'd be already clipping hyacinth's frail foliage
and muttering about summer's late arrival and the dallying west
    winds.
Likewise, his bees were first to breed, first to swarm,
140 and first to gather honey and have it spilling from the comb.
He had lime trees and a wealth of shrubs in flower,
and as many as the blossoms with which each tree
bedecked itself early in the year was the number ripening
    later on.
He'd been known in his day to set in rows elms that were well
    grown,
a hardy pear, and thorns already bearing sloes,
a plane tree that provided shade for drinking under.
The like of this, however, I must forgo—time and space
    conspiring
to defeat me—and leave for later men to make more of.

    So listen now, while I outline the qualities bestowed on bees by
    Jupiter
150 as his reward for their attention to the Curetes'

songlike sounds, their shields clashing like cymbals,
and for nourishing our king of heaven in that Cretan cave.*
  They alone share the care of their young and live united in one
      house,
and lead lives subject to the majesty of law.
They alone recognize the full worth of home and homeland.
Mindful that winter follows, they set to work in summer
and store what they acquire for the common good.
Some are responsible for food and by a fixed agreement
keep busy in the fields, others stay within the walls
and lay down as the first foundation of the comb the tear of a   160
      narcissus
and sticky resin from the bark of trees from which they then
      suspend the clinging honey cells.
  Others are appointed to bring up the young, the future of the
      race,
while others still pack the honey, the purest honey,
and stuff the cells with perfect nectar. Some,
allotted to be sentries at the alighting boards,
take turns to keep an eye on clouds and coming rain
and to relieve the homing bees of their burdens, or, having
      rounded up a troop,
keep out the drones, that lazy shower, from the mangers.
Full steam ahead! The honey smacks of fragrant thyme.
  The same as when the Cyclopes hammered thunderbolts   170
from stubborn lumps of ore, some worked the bullhide bellows
      out and in
to fan the give and take of breezes, and others dipped the
      bronze
to sizzle in the trough, while Etna groaned beneath the weight of
      anvils;*
as one, they flex the muscles of their arms in rhythm, upwards
      and down,
and keep the iron that's being turned gripped tightly in their
      tongs.
  So, if it's all right to liken little things to great,
an innate love of ownership impels the bees of Cecrops

each through his own responsibility. The elders' cares include
the fortifying of the comb and moulding of intricate shelters.
180 Come night, the youngsters haul themselves back home,
  exhausted,
leg-baskets loaded down with thyme; they pick randomly on
  wild strawberry,
the blue-grey willow, spurge laurel (that's the bee plant),
  blushing saffron,
and a luxury of limes and lindens and lilies tinted rust.
As one they rest; as one they work.
Come morning, and a hurry from the hives, all go and no delay,
until the evening star suggests that they return from where
they're gleaning and retire. Then they head home, where they
  attend to themselves.
You'll hear a hum—their mumble thickening around the doors
and on the doorsteps—until afterwards when they've settled in
  their chambers
190 and a stillness reigns, and well-earned sleep overtakes their
  weary limbs.
  Nor will they stray far from the hives when rain is on its way
or trust the weather in the face and force of an east wind,
but from the safety of the walls they venture on brief sorties
to fetch a drop of water and, often, little pebbles—
the way a skimpy boat tossed here and there in the waves' mercy
takes on a load of ballast—to steady themselves as they fly high as
  pleases them.
  In fact they have another habit—you'll wonder how it ever
  did find favour—
that is, that bees refrain from intercourse, their bodies never
weaken into the ways of love, nor suffer pangs of labour.
200 Instead, themselves, they pick their young up in their mouths
from leaves and lovely meadows; all by themselves, they'll
  supply
the city with a queen and little citizens, and so maintain the royal
  court and realm of wax.
  Often, too, while wandering, they'll graze their wings on
  jagged rocks

and beneath their burden pay the final sacrifice—
such is their love for flowers and pride in the production of the
     honey.
Therefore, although there's but brief life allotted to each one of
     them
(the most they have is seven summers), their kind can't be killed
     off
and, years on top of years, their houses stay in good standing
and their ancestral rolls include grandfathers of their fathers.
     What's more, there was not in Egypt or the whole of Lydia,   210
nor among the Parthians or the Medes,* such regard for royalty.
When their queen's safe and sound, they're all at peace.
But when she dies their trust is shredded, and they take to
     wrecking
honey halls and sacking well-wrought honeycombs.
Of all they do, she is the patron—that's why they all look up to
and surround her, bustling with a loud hubbub.
Sometimes they'll hold her up on high; for her they'll lay down
     lives
and count it a death with honour, the one from wounds in battle.
     By such signs, and on foot of such examples,
some say that bees have supped a draught that is divine,   220
that, as a matter of true fact, a god pervades the whole wide
     world,
sea's expanse and heaven's height,
whence flocks and herds and men, and all species of savage beast,
derive that fine line of life the second they are born.
And, what's more, to him all things return in time, dissolved
and reabsorbed; there is no place for death—instead they soar,
still alive—to take their rightful place among the stars.
     If you happen ever to broach the storehouse where they hoard
     the honey
be sure you have first washed your mouth out with a sup of
     water,
then surround your seeing fingers with smoke to still and settle   230
     them.
Twice in the year men harvest honey,

once, when Taÿgete of the Seven Sisters* shows the world her
    comely face
and spurns the ocean currents with a shrug,
and again when, trying to escape from Pisces,* she slides down
    the sky
beneath the waves, a sorry sight, and drowns.
    There's no end to the wrath of bees—vexed, they'll inflame
        their stings
with poison and, fastening to a vein, deposit darts that you can't
    see—
inflicting harm, they'll forfeit their own lives.
    But if you fear a winter will be hard, and would look out for
    them,
240 in pity for their bruised and battered spirit, a state brought to its
    knees,
who would hesitate to purify the hive with smoking heads of
    thyme
and lop off useless cells, for oftentimes an eft, unnoticed, has
    been gnawing
at the comb, or the nest's a mess of cockroaches that shun the
    light,
and there's a drone—that good-for-nothing—squatting down
    to scoff another's feed.
Or a savage hornet has entered in the fray with its unfair
    advantage,
or the dreaded moth, or, just as bad, a spider, Minerva's fateful
    enemy,*
has slung its fatal web across the frame.
The more trials sent to test them, the keener they become, one
    and all,
to throw themselves into the mending of their tumbled
    world.
250 They re-stock the rows, and weave the store's new walls with
    fruit of flowers.
    If, in fact, life brings to bees the same misfortunes as to us
their bodies may fall faint with grievous illness
whose signs you'll have no trouble recognizing.

The minute they grow sick their colour changes, a haggard look
    disfigures features,
and they carry out into the open those whose life's light is
    quenched,
a sorrowful procession, and either hang around
the threshold, their feet tucked up beneath them,
or shuffle slowly in the temple,
the all of them weak with the hunger and perished with the
    cold.
Then you hear a deeper sound, drawn out,   260
the way the south winds rumbled once through frozen forests,
the way a troubled sea shrieks and creaks at ebb-tide;
or a raging fire roars in a furnace with the door shut tight.
  When things have come to this I recommend you light
    galbanum for its scent,
and pipe in honey through a reed, going to no end of bother
to encourage them, the worn and weary ones, and coax them
    back to food they know and love.
It will help to have a blend of pounded galls, those acrid oak-
    apples,
with dried leaves of roses, or must reduced a long time
over an open flame, and raisins from the Psythian vine,
thyme from Athens, and pungent centaury.   270
And growing in the meadows there's a flower farmers call
    'amellus',*
that is star wort, and it's not hard to find, for it raises from a
    single root
a veritable forest—itself is golden-lined
but in the petals it produces so abundantly
a purple glow shimmers through deep violet.
Many's the time it's been employed to decorate the altars of the
    gods.
Its taste is bitter. Shepherds pick it in
the close-cropped valleys along the winding Mella.
Take my word. Boil its roots in a strong-smelling wine
and serve it to the bees in baskets left beside their doorways.   280

It can happen in a flash that someone's stock completely fails—
and he can see no way to supplant it with new blood.
Time then to let you in on what that great Arcadian keeper
first discovered,* that is—this happened often—that putrid
    blood
of slaughtered cattle brought new swarms into being.
    Listen. I'll tell all from the root to bloom, share all I've heard.
For where Pellaean people live their happy lives beside Canopus
    on the Nile*
whose flowing waters form floodpools
on which they do their rounds in brightly painted pinnaces
290 and where the Persians, race of archers, crowd in close as
    neighbours,
and a tumbling torrent splits into its seven deltas—
the river, which has travelled all the way from the land of sun-
    bronzed Ethiopians
and which fertilizes fertile Egypt with dank sands—that's where
the continued well-being of the bees rests safe and surely on the
    skill I've promised to describe.

First they choose an area, a place made smaller for this very
    purpose,
enclosed with roof tiles and its walls pressed in.
Then they add four apertures that face four quarters
of the wind and admit a slanting light.
Then they'll pick a bull calf out, his two years' growth of horn a
    crown upon his brow,
300 and plug his nostrils and, despite the fight he'll offer, put a stop
    to his breathing.
And when he's been assailed with blows, and while his hide
is still unbroken, they'll pummel to a pulp his flesh.
    That's how they leave him, shut away in that enclosure,
    beneath his ribcage
piles of branches, thyme, and newly picked spurge laurel.
All this proceeds while west winds first play on the waves,
before spring restores a flush of colour to the face of fields,
before the chattering swallow attaches her nest to the rafters.

Meanwhile, the bullock's tender bones begin to heat and
    ferment
and—astonishing to see—strange animals appear,
with, at first, no feet to speak of, then with wings whirring,   310
as they mill around on their play flights, first here, then there,
and then spill out like heavy showers poured from summer
    clouds,
or like those arrows the lightly armed Parthians unleash from
    bows
to strike the first blows in battle.
   O Muses, say what god was it
who with this miracle advanced the minds of men?

The shepherd, Aristaeus, turned his back on Tempe, through
    which the Peneius flows*—
or so the story goes—his bees all lost to hunger and disease,
and stood heartsore and sorry at the sacred river's source
and, in words like these, directed his complaint to the one who   320
    bore him,*
'Mother of mine, Mother Cyrene, whose home is in the depths
of this deep water, how could you bear me to this noble line of
    gods—
(if it's true, as you assert, Apollo is my father)—
for fate itself to turn against me? Oh, whither has your love for
    me been driven?
Why did you teach me to reach up my hopes to heaven?
Look! Even this distinction of my mortal being,
hard won by me through expert care of crops and cattle
and nothing stinted, and even with you for a mother, I must
    give up.
Then why not, while you're at it, uproot with your own hands
    my fruiting forests,
burn down my stalls, wipe out the harvest I have won,   330
set fire to all that I have in the ground, and launch attacks on my
    vines
with a battleaxe, if you have grown so displeased with any good
    I've done.'

Deep in the river,* in her chamber, his mother listened to his
    cry,
while all around her, carding fleeces from Miletus,
all of them dyed bottle blue, were nymphs
whose names are Drymo, Xantho, Ligea, and Phyllodoce,
337 fair heads of hair cascading down their shining necks [. . .]
339 and Cydippe, and fairhaired Lycorias, the one a maiden still,
340 the other fresh from pangs of labour, her first nativity,
and there was Clio and her sister Beroe, the two of them the
       daughters of Oceanus,
the two of them bedecked with gold and both dressed up in
       coloured skins,
and there was Ephyre and Opis and Asian Deiopeia,
and fleet-footed Arethusa, her bow and arrows put away at last.
And in their midst was Clymene, rambling on about
Vulcan's efforts all in vain and Mars' deception and the joy he
      stole,*
elaborating all the loves of all the gods, from Chaos' time to
      ours.*
    And as they sat enthralled, winding soft wool from the
      spindle,
Aristaeus' mourning made its way again into his mother's
      ear
350 and all of them, seated on their crystal chairs, were paralysed,
      struck dumb—
till Arethusa, before any of the others,
raised her golden head above the water to find the sorrow's
      source
and cried out from afar, 'Oh, not for nothing has a sigh caused
      you such fright,
sister Cyrene, for it is he, poor Aristaeus, who's nearest and most
      dear to you,
who is standing by the waters of our father Peneius, a well of
      tears,
and he's naming you the hard-hearted one.'
His mother then, her mind wild with new feeling, called,
'Yes, bring him, bring him over here, he has a right to walk

where the gods walk.' And at once she bade the waters part
and made a pathway for her son's passage.   360
Then all around him waves crested like mountain peaks
and, safe in that embrace, bore him below the water.

   And now, in wonder of his mother's home, her watery
        realm,
pools forming part of caverns and gurgling groves,
he wanders, astounded by majestic movements of the water,
rivers rippling under earth's great dome and reaching out
in all directions—one called Phasis, and another Lycus,
and the source from which the deep Enipeus makes its first
        appearance,
and from which father Tiber, and Anio, come streaming,
and rattling down through rocks, Hypanis, and Caicus of   370
        Mysia,
and that river that wears a bull's expression, and gilded horns,
Eridanus, than which no river throws itself more forcefully
through rich farmlands into shining sea.

   Then, when he reached his mother's chamber, its hanging
        softstone roof,
and Cyrene had recognized his idle tears,
his sisters formed a line to offer him
spring water for his hands and special cloths to dry them.
Others piled the table high with dishes for the feast
and kept refilling goblets, while others still fuelled the altar fires
        with incense from Arabia.
His mother then spoke out, 'Raise up your glasses, let's drink a 380
        toast of wine
to Oceanus.'* And then to him, of everything the father,
she said her private prayer, and to the sisterhood of nymphs,
guardians of a hundred forests, and a hundred rivers, too.
And then three times she sprinkled nectar on the sacred hearth,
three times a flame flared to the ceiling, giving out its light,
a sign to lift the heart, and then she spoke these words:
'Deep in Carpathian woods, there is a prophet by the name of
        Proteus,*
who is the colour of the sea, who travels the wide watery range

pulled by a team that's one half fish, the other half two-leggèd
    horse.

390 And as we speak, he is returning to the havens of Emathia and
    Pallene,
the place where he was born—it's him, we nymphs
and even agèd Nereus,* revere, for everything is known
to that seer—whatever was, what is, and all that is to come.
(For this is just what Neptune wanted—whose herds
of fulsome seals he pastures underneath the waves.)
He's the one that you, my son, must bind in chains
so he'll explain the sorry story of the cause of sickness and bring
    it to a good conclusion.
If he's not forced he'll tell you nothing,
nor will you bring him round by begging. Brute strength
    alone

400 will grind him down and run his useless wiles aground.
I myself, when the sun has turned noon's heat full up,
when grasses shrivel and herds appreciate the shade,
will bring you to the old man's private quarters where he
    retreats
exhausted from work in the waves, where you'll be able to accost
    him as he lies asleep.
But even when you've grabbed a hold of him and fettered him
he'll conjure different forms and features of wild animals to foil
    you.
One minute he'll become a bristling boar, a shady tiger,
scaly snake, or lion with its tawny mane,
or burst into a whiff of flame to slough off his chains,

410 or melt into thin air—and away with him!
But the more he plies his repertoire of shapes,
my son, the more you must maintain a grip
till his physique reverts and so resumes the profile
you first set eyes on when you found him, draped beneath the
    weight of sleep.'
    And after she had said her say, she poured a perfume of
    ambrosia
and covered her son's body, tip to toe, so that

from the hairs of his combed head a sweet essence emanated
and strength returned to his nimble limbs.

                                            Etched into a
    mountainside,
there's an enormous cavern where wave on wave
driven by the wind shatters itself in the recesses,   420
time after time the safest shelter for sailors waylaid in a storm.
That's where you'll find this Proteus—hiding behind a shield of
    rock.
  And there, just there the nymph instructs the boy to lie in
    ambush
when it's dark, while she stands hard by hidden in a mist.
The Dog Star by this time was all ablaze, burning up the sky and
    leaving the people of the Indies
parched with the thirst, and the fiery sun had gobbled
half his daily course,* the grasses wilted and withered, and the
    shrivelled river beds,
their dried-up channels, were baked to dust by its beams' burn.
  While Proteus was making from the waves to the cave,
as was his wont, round about him ran the race of mermen   430
and splashed the briny spray here, there and everywhere.
Seals lay about along the shore and settled down to sleep,
while he, the master, like that herdsman in the mountains,*
when twilight draws young cattle from the outfields
and the lambs' baa-ing grabs the wolves' attention,
sat himself down on a rock and took stock of every one of them.
  Aristaeus saw his chance—and seized it.
He scarcely gave the old man a split second to compose his tired
    self,
but rushed in with a roar and slapped the chains on him
before he could get up. But he, to nature true and conscious of   440
    his powers,
transformed himself into the weirdest things—
fire, or a fearsome beast, or rushing stream—
but of these ruses none succeeded in securing his escape
and, subjugated, he resumed his former and first self, and then,
    with a human's voice,

spoke up, and asked, 'Who ordered you, most bold of youths,
to break into our homes, what do you want of me?' And
Aristaeus answered,
'But, Proteus, you know, it's well you know, for nothing can be
lost on you;
desist, and don't pretend otherwise. I come, instructed by the
gods,
to find an answer and a reason for what has left me weary and
worn out.'
450   That's all he said. At this, at last, the seer turned his sea-green
eyes
and stared at him. Then, grinding his teeth hard,
he opened up to explain his destiny,
'Don't think they don't have gods' support, the angers you are
weighted with,
you're paying for a grievous offence. For it is Orpheus,* the
pitiful,
who is handing down this punishment, by no means as much as
you deserve,
had fate not stood in the way, for his bitter rage about his bride's
abduction.
It's true, in hasty flight from you, she failed to see—
doomed as she was—hiding in tall grass and right in front of
her,
the seven-headed serpent, a sentry on the river bank.
460 Then the chorus of her peers, the Dryads,* filled the
mountaintops with their lament,
the heights of Rhodope cried out, too, in mourning,
as did lofty Pangaea, and the land of warring Rhesus,
and the Getae, the river Hebrus and the princess Orithyia.
   'Heartsick and sore, Orpheus sought consolation on his lyre,
a hollowed tortoiseshell.* Of you, sweet wife, of you, he sang his
sorry song,
all lonesome on the shore, at dawning of the day, of you, at day's
decline, of you.
He risked even the gorge of Taenarus,* the towering portals of
the underworld,

and the abode of spirits where darkness reigns like a dismal fog;
these he passed through to approach the shades and their
    scaresome lord,
those hearts that don't know how to be swayed by human pleas   470
    for prayers.
But, unsettled by his singing, from the nether reach of
    Hell,
came insubstantial phantoms, like those who have lived long
    away from light,
teeming like the countless birds that lurk among the leaves
until, at evening time, winter rains herd them home from the
    hills,
mothers and men, the build of once big-hearted heroes,
now dead and done with; boys, too, and unwed girls,
and youths borne on their funeral pyres before their parents'
    eyes—
around whom lay the clabber, and disfigured reed beds by
    Cocytus, that kept them
locked in, among stagnant pools and murky marshes,
and the Styx' nine coils that kept them prisoner.   480
Instead they froze, spellbound, Death's inner rooms and depths
    of Tartarus,
the Furies, too, their hair a knot of writhing snakes,
and gawking Cerberus stopped in his tracks, his three mouths
    open wide,
and Ixion's wheel, wind-propelled, settled to a standstill.*
  'And now, on his way home, he had avoided every pitfall,
and Eurydice, restored to him and trailing close behind (as
    Proserpina
had decreed),* was emerging into heaven's atmosphere
when a stroke of madness caught him, who loved her, off his
    guard—
a pardonable offence, you'd think, if the Dead knew how to
    pardon.
He stopped, and for a moment wasn't thinking—no!—   490
Eurydice was his again and on the brink of light, and who knows
    what possessed him

but he turned back to look. Like that, his efforts were undone,
    and the pacts he'd entered
with that tyrant had dissolved. Three peals of thunder clapped
    across that paludal hell.
"What," she cried, "what wretched luck has ruined me—and
    you, O Orpheus,
what burning need? Look, cold-hearted fate is calling me
again; sleep draws its curtain on my brimming eyes.
And so, farewell, I'm carried off in night's immense embrace,
and now reach out my hands to you in vain—for I am yours no
    more."
    'So she spoke, and suddenly, like wisps of smoke, she vanished
500 in thin air. She watched him for the final time, while he,
with so much still to say, attempted to cling on to shadows.
No longer would the ferryman permit him cross
the marshy pool that lay between them.*
What was left for him to do? Where could he turn, his wife now
    taken
twice from him? Would any wailing move the shades—or please
    the gods?
Already she was making her stiff way across the Styx.
    'For seven whole long months, they say, one following the
    other,
he slumped in mourning, alone beneath a towering cliff, by the
    waterside of Strymon,
expounding under frozen stars his broken-hearted threnody
510 to the delight of tigers, and even drew the oak to him with his
    style of singing,
just as a nightingale will sorrow under poplar shade
for her lost brood which some brute ploughboy spotted
and pilfered from the nest, though it was not yet fledged.
That bird still weeps by night and, perched in a tree, repeats
her plaintive keen, filling far and wide with the ache of her
    heartbreak.
No thought of love, or marriage, could distract him.
Disconsolate, through icefields of the north, the snow-kissed
    river Tanais,

and the Riphaean range whose peaks are never free from frost,
he drifted, lamenting lost Eurydice and Pluto's broken boon.
But the bacchantes thought themselves scorned by such   520
     devotion
and, one night of rites and revelling,
tore him apart, this youth, and broadcast the pieces through the
     land.*
Even then, sundered from a neck as pale as marble
and carried in the current down the Hebrus,
that voice, that stone-cold tongue, continued to cry out,
"Eurydice, O poor Eurydice," as its life's blood drained out of it
and the river banks repeated that "Eurydice", a dolorous
     refrain.'

Thus spoke Proteus,* and then he plunged into the sea
and where he plunged an eddy swirled down in the wave.
But not Cyrene. Unasked, she uttered to her trembling   530
     audience:
'My son, cast off the burden of your cares
for here's the reason for the sickness of your bees
and this is why the nymphs with whom Eurydice danced in the
     groves
brought rack and ruin to the hives. So you, a supplicant,
must make an offering, with peace the aim,
and pray, and pay respect in atonement to the gracious nymphs.
And in response they'll grant forgiveness and repeal their rage.
     'The way to supplicate I will first tell:
select four bulls, superior in form and frame,
such as you've grazing now on lush uplands of Lycaeus,   540
and an equal count of heifers, whose neck no yoke has ever
     touched;
erect for these four altars by the tall temples of the goddesses,
lance them, and let the sacred blood spill from their throats,
and leave these carcasses abandoned in a leafy den.
And later, when nine days have dawned, you'll send as offerings
     to Orpheus
soporific poppies, and sacrifice a ewe that's black,

then go back to the thicket and worship with a slaughtered calf
Eurydice, who by now will be appeased.'

                      And with no halt or
    hesitation
he did all that his mother bid.* Come to the temple, he raised the
    altars as prescribed,
550 led in four bulls, superior in form and frame,
and an equal count of heifers, whose neck no yoke has ever
    touched.
And later, when nine days have dawned, he sends his offerings
to Orpheus and goes back to the thicket . . .
And there they met a miracle and looked it in the face—
from those cattle's decomposing flesh, the hum of bees,
bubbling first, then boiling over and, trailing giant veils into the
    trees,
they hung like grapes in bunches from the swaying branches.

Such was the song* that I took on to sing, about the care of
    crops
and stock, and trees with fruit, while he, our mighty Caesar,
560 was going hell for leather along the great Euphrates
adding victory to triumph, winning the war for people who
    appreciate his deeds,
and laying down the law—enough to earn his place in heaven.
    And I, Virgil, was lying in the lap of Naples, quite at home
in studies of the arts of peace, I, who once amused myself
with rustic rhymes, and, still a callow youth,
sang of you, Tityrus, as I lounged beneath the reach of one great
    beech.

EXPLANATORY NOTES

BOOK ONE

7–18 *O Liber . . . O god of Tegea*: Virgil adds gods and culture heroes from Greek tradition. *Liber*: Bacchus. *Neptune . . . a snorting horse*: in their mythical contest to be divine patron of Athens, Poseidon/Neptune offered the horse, which sprang from the ground at a blow from his trident, while Athene/Minerva won with her offering of the olive tree. *patron of shady woods . . . chaparral of Ceos*: Aristaeus of Ceos, son of the nymph Cyrene and Apollo, seen here as shepherd, but he was also honoured as a cult hero or discoverer of arable farming and beekeeping (cf. note to 4.283–4 and 4.327–31: he will be the farmer's model hero who overcomes disaster by patience and perseverance in Book 4. *Pan . . . Tegea*: Pan, the Greek god of herds, came from Arcadia, whose chief city was Tegea, and he was worshipped on its mountains Lycaeus and Maenalus.

19 *that youth, too, creator of the crooked plough*: the first of three references (see also lines 39 and 166) to the myth of Demeter/Ceres which was celebrated in the mysteries of Eleusis near Athens. The youth is Triptolemos (also called Iacchus), the baby whom Demeter tried to make immortal when she acted as his nurse during her time on earth seeking for her kidnapped daughter Persephone/Proserpina. Interrupted by his anxious mother, she gave the mortal Triptolemos the power to invent the plough and so create agriculture.

24 *you too, O Caesar*: Octavian had named his own adoptive father Caesar as a god after his death, and so was expected to join the gods himself in due course. Virgil follows the mythical tradition which divided the universe into three divine kingdoms, assigning Jupiter earth and sky, Neptune the sea, and Dis the underworld. The poet of the countryside naturally stresses that Octavian may be 'in charge of countryside . . . begetter of the harvest or as master of the seasons' (lines 26–7), and alludes (line 28, 'a garland of your mother's myrtle') to the myrtle as flower of Venus, who as mother of Aeneas was ancestress of the Julian family.

31 *Tethys forfeits all her waves to have you as a son-in-law*: here, Octavian is assimilated to Achilles, son of the sea-nymph Thetis.

32 *you will add a new star to the zodiac*: as Julius Caesar was identified with the comet seen after his death, so his son Octavian may be deified as a constellation: the old version of the zodiac assigned two segments to the Scorpion and its Claws, until the Claws were replaced by Libra in honour of Octavian, born on 23 September.

36–9 *let not the nether world of Tartarus . . . she hears her calling her*: the underworld offered the virtuous a blessed afterlife in the Elysian fields, which was also the reward of initiates in the Eleusinian mysteries. The mysteries assimilated the grain beneath the earth to Proserpina, who stayed with her husband Dis in winter and returned only for part of each year.

62–3 *Deucalion cast . . . a hardy race!*: Deucalion and his wife Pyrrha were the only survivors when Jupiter's great flood destroyed mankind. They were instructed by the oracle of the goddess Themis to throw stones behind them which became the new race of men, hard(y) like stones.

102–3 *Mysia . . . Gargarus*: here and elsewhere (e.g. line 120, 'Strymon cranes' from Thrace), Virgil uses exotic lands as a foil for his celebration of Italy. Mysia and Gargarus were in north-west Anatolia, near Troy, Rome's original city.

149 *Dodona*: in Epirus, the site of a famous oracle of Zeus/Jupiter, which gave prophecy from its oak trees, the source of acorns, man's first primitive food (cf. 'acorns of Epirus', line 8).

166 *Iacchus' marvellous riddle*: another allusion to the symbolic use of farm tools (here a winnowing fan) in the mysteries at Eleusis. Cf. line 19 and note.

204 *sky formations*: most of these constellations are still known by Virgil's names, but note that Taurus (line 217) is gilt-horned as if an ox adorned for sacrifice; the Seven Sisters (line 221) are the Pleiades, and the Star of Knossos (line 222) identifies Ariadne, princess of Crete, whom Bacchus took as his consort and honoured by setting her crown in the sky.

233 *Five spheres make up the heavens*: these are the celestial zones reflected in the division of the earth between glacial poles, intolerable equatorial heat, and the two temperate zones habitable by men. Virgil is adapting the poetic description of the Alexandrian geographer Eratosthenes (fr. 16 Powell), also known to Lucretius, who interpreted the nature of the earth more pessimistically (Lucretius, 5.195–205).

242–3 *its counterpart/lies underfoot*: this account (with lines 247–51) seems to blend the idea of the Antipodes on the opposite side of the globe (whose night is our day) with the Stygian underworld beneath the earth (cf. lines 36–9).

244–5 *the sky's enormous serpent . . . the Big and Little Dipper*: these are the polar constellations Draco (line 205) and the Great and Lesser Bear (cf. 'Lycaon's child', line 138, referring to Callisto daughter of Lycaon, who with her son was transformed by Jupiter into the two constellations). Cf. line 246 ('that disdain to be touched'): viewed from Mediterranean latitudes, the constellations were always above the night horizon, and so were interpreted by myth as never sinking into the surrounding Ocean. From Homer onwards Greeks and Romans knew these constellations by both the mythical names and a homely alternative: what we call the Big Dipper they called 'the waggon'.

276 *days suitable for certain work*: Virgil is offering a pastiche of Hesiod's teachings about lucky and unlucky days of the month, which were numbered by the phases of the moon. 'Beware the fifth': cf. *Works and Days* 802.) But he has conflated several of the monstrous enemies of the Olympian gods, the Titans, Coeus, and Iapetus (*Theogony* 134 f.), Typhoeus (821), children of Earth, and the brothers Otus and Ephialtes (*Odyssey* 11.305–20). Homer had both Pelion and Ossa, the great Thessalian mountains, heaped on Olympus. Virgil's variation reverses this.

332 *Athos, Rhodope, and the peaks of Ceraunia*: Athos is in the Greek peninsula of Pallene, Rhodope in Thrace, and Ceraunia a mountain range on the north-west coast of the Greek peninsula nearest to Italy.

404–5 *Nisus comes into view . . . she stole*: Nisus, king of Megara, was betrayed to his enemy Minos by his daughter Scylla, who cut off his magic lock of purple hair. Minos rejected her and both Scylla and Nisus were turned into sea-birds: she became a shearwater (*ciris*). The story is told by Ovid (*Metamorphoses* 8) and in the short pseudo-Virgilian epic *Ciris*.

437 *Glaucus . . . and Ino's son, Melicertes*: the human fisherman Glaucus became a sea-god; Ino, aunt of Bacchus, was driven mad by Hera/Juno and jumped into the sea with her son Melicertes. They became sea-gods and protectors of sailors. At Rome they were worshipped as the goddess Mater Matuta and the god Portunus.

466 *that time that Caesar fell*: historians reported dreadful portents both before and after the assassination of Caesar, but the solar eclipse referred to here occurred six months after Caesar's death, in October 44. 'Infidels' (line 468) marks the sins against the gods of Rome's civil wars, assimilated to the iron age of conflict within the family and country denounced by Virgil's predecessor Catullus, and later Ovid.

489–90 *Philippi observed . . . in a civil war*: the battle of Philippi in Macedonian Thrace in 42 BCE, when Octavian and Antony defeated the forces of Caesar's killers, Brutus and Cassius, is deliberately assimilated to the battle fought at Pharsalus in Thessaly at which Caesar defeated Pompey and the Republican forces six years earlier, in 48.

492 *Emathia*: a region of Thessaly.

Haemus: a Thracian mountain range; cf. 2.488.

502 *the lies Laomedon told at Troy*: Laomedon, king of Troy, deceived Neptune and Apollo into building him defensive walls around Troy and then reneged on his payment. He also cheated Hercules of his reward for killing the sea-monster sent by Neptune, and was punished, first when Hercules captured and sacked the city, and later, posthumously, when the Greeks again took the city under his grandson Priam. It was part of Augustan ideology to stress the guilt of Troy as one cause of Rome's own sufferings in the civil war.

512–14 *chariots . . . no control*: representing Rome's young leader as a charioteer will have appealed to popular admiration for these races, but may have suggested either of two Greek traditions. It is more likely that Virgil was alluding to the Platonic allegory comparing the moral aspect of the soul to a charioteer who must control his unruly horses of spirit and base appetite (see Plato, *Phaedrus* 253d–254e), than to the cautionary tale of Phaethon, who tried to drive the chariot of his father, the Sun, and caused a conflagration on earth.

BOOK TWO

15 *the groves of Jupiter*: his oracle at Dodona.

16 *the other one*: Virgil is distinguishing two varieties of oak: the English oak (*quercus*) and the durmast oak (*aesculus*).

18 *laurels of Parnassus*: Delphi, on Mt. Parnassus, was the prophetic shrine of Apollo, and leaves of his tree, the laurel, were chewed by the Pythoness for inspiration.

37–8 *Ismarus . . . Taburnus*: here and repeatedly in Book 2 Virgil combines and contrasts exotic places (Ismarus is a mountain range in Thrace) with Italian sites like Taburnus in Samnium.

87 *orchards of Alcinous*: the king of mythical Phaeacia, whose gardens and orchards are described in *Odyssey* 7.112–32.

88 *Crustumine . . . Tarentine*: from Crustumerium and Tarentum, in different regions of Italy.

90–5 *Lesbos . . . Rhaetia*: again Virgil lists popular wines from around the Mediterranean, the islands of Lesbos, Thasos, Chios, and Rhodes, and Egypt and Lydia (western Turkey). *Lagean* (line 93), from the Lagid dynasty of Ptolemies who ruled Egypt, alludes to Egyptian wine. Rhaetia (line 95) is the Roman name for Alto Adige and Tyrol, and this wine was a favourite of Augustus, according to Suetonius (*Augustus* 77). In contrast, Virgil cites *Falernian* (line 97), and wine from Aminnea (line 97), both from Italian Campania, as superior to the wines of Lydian Mt. Tmolus and Phanae in Chios.

105–7 *how many grains . . . how many waves*: Virgil's first comparison echoes a famous poem of Catullus (Cat. 7), measuring the kisses he wants from his Lesbia by the uncountable sands of Libya, but he has substituted the waves of the Adriatic for Catullus' second allusion to the countless stars of the sky.

114–15 *the ends of earth . . . Scythian tribes*: this choice of climatic opposites anticipates the fuller accounts of North Africa and Scythia in 3.339–83.

116–21 *the Indies . . . Chinese*: the Romans knew of these lands beyond their own empire only indirectly from the middlemen who traded spices from Arabia (Virgil names them with the Latin form of the name Sheba), rare wood like ebony from the Indian peoples of South Asia, cotton from East Africa, and silk from China. These places will be recalled in lines 136–9, where the Lydian river Hermus is cited for the gold panned from its stream.

126–7 *the citron . . . product of Media*: Virgil gives special treatment to the citron (*malus Medica*) as a cure-all against poison, bad breath, and breathlessness. Romans of his time identified the ancient Medes (line 134) with their contemporary enemies, the Parthians. Here and elsewhere in Book 2 he is drawing on the Greek botanist Theophrastus, and Pliny quotes him and partly corrects him in *Natural History* 11.278.

140–2 *no oxen . . . serries of spears*: the fire-breathing oxen and warriors born from dragon's teeth of mythical Colchis (and Thebes). Italy is free of mythical monsters, as it is less plausibly said to be of wild beasts and poisonous plants.

146 *Clitumnus*: a lake with sacred springs in Umbria where white oxen were bred for sacrifice to Jupiter and other gods at Rome.

159–62 *Larius . . . Lucrine*: praise of the northern lakes Maggiore and Garda is combined with praise for Agrippa's recent engineering feat of linking Lake Avernus and the Lucrine lake in Campania to the Tyrrhenian coast to provide an inland naval basin. His artificial harbour is also praised by Propertius (3.18), writing soon after 23 BCE, but seems to have been abandoned within a generation.

167–8 *Marsians . . . Volscian lancers*: hill peoples of central Italy subdued by Rome and long since incorporated in her Italian confederation. The Ligurians from the north-west were brought under control in the second century BCE.

169–70 *Decii . . . Scipios*: in listing Roman military heroes Virgil is not bound by chronology; the Decii won great victories over the Samnites and Etruscans in the fourth and third centuries: Camillus conquered Veii and defeated the Gauls at the beginning of the fourth century, the elder Scipio (Africanus Maior) defeated Carthage at the end of the third century and his adoptive grandson (Aemilianus) destroyed the city in 146 BCE. Only Marius is recent, and he is mentioned here not only because he conquered Jugurtha of Numidia and defeated the Teutones and Cimbri, but as husband of Julius Caesar's aunt, he was virtually an ancestor of Octavian.

170–2 *Caesar . . . rebuffs the craven Indian*: this may refer to diplomatic overtures from India. It goes beyond any campaigning by Octavian or his deputies during the years 36–29 BCE when the *Georgics* were being written.

224–5 *Capua . . . Acerrae*: Capua was chief city of Campania, the most sunny and fertile region of Italy with rich volcanic soils on the slopes of Vesuvius. The river Clanius and town of Acerrae are in the same region.

277–8 *run parallel/ and still maintain right angles*: the vines should be arrayed like legionary soldiers, with those in alternate rows placed midway between those in the previous row so that the distance between individuals is equal in all directions—the *quincunx* formation.

325 *almighty father, Air, marries the earth*: the fertilizing union of sky and earth called the *hieros gamos*, or sacred marriage: Lucretius (1.250–3) also represents spring fertility as the union of father sky and mother earth; both may go back to Homer's description of the union of Zeus and Hera on an open hillside in *Iliad* 14.346–51.

380–9 *And they're the why . . . tender tokens*: tradition (reported by Varro in his *De re rustica* and his scholarly works on the history of drama) was that the Athenians (whose first king was Theseus) sacrificed a goat (*tragos*) to Dionysus in atonement for the damage done to his vines and performed the first tragedies (*tragos* + *ōdē* = goatsong). Compare Horace, *Art of Poetry* 220: 'The man who competed with tragic poetry on account of the worthless he-goat . . .' Virgil's account of the adoption of this custom by Italians is recalled by Horace in his 'Letter to Augustus' (*Epistles* 2.1), 139–67: 'The farmers of old, sturdy and happy with a small stock, after storing the harvest, easing their bodies at a time of festival, and their spirits enduring hardship in hope of its end, along with their sons and workmates, and their loyal wives made sacrifice to earth with a pig and Sylvanus with milk . . .'

437–8 *boxwood . . . stands of pine near Narycum*: Virgil first recalls Catullus 4, spoken by his yacht made of exotic box from the south coast of the Black Sea, then pairs it with pitch pine forests close to a small town in south Italy.

448 *Ituraean bows*: named from a people in northern Palestine. Only foreign, usually eastern, troops were archers, and their bows also came from the east.

452 *swarms of bees*: besides recalling a variety of trees, Virgil is setting the scene for the theme of Book 4.

456 *the maddened Centaurs*: a Greek myth (see *Odyssey* 21.295–304 and Ovid, *Metamorphoses* 12.210–535) told how Pirithous, king of the Lapiths in Thessaly, invited his neighbours the Centaurs to his wedding but they could not hold their drink and when one of them tried to kidnap the bride there was a great battle.

This is the first of a series of Thessalian legends invoked by Virgil, many associated with horse-breeding.

487 *Spercheus . . . Taygetus*: both idyllic wild places are Greek: the river Spercheus is Thessalian, the mountains near Sparta. The young women of Sparta exercised with men and were thought of as fearless hunters, but 'the one who'd lay me down to rest' in the next sentence is not a Spartan maiden but some imaginary deity who will transport Virgil to Thracian Haemus.

490 *That man*: the poet surely alludes here to Lucretius, who was proud of saving men from the fear of Hell by his Epicurean teaching that gods did

not punish men for their sins and there was no afterlife. Lucretius also denounced the greed and political ambition which led to civil war at Rome (cf. Lucretius 3.59–73) in language close to Virgil's denunciation in lines 495–511.

493–4 *with country gods—/Pan and old Sylvanus*: cf. 1.16 and 20, and note. Sylvanus, god of the uncleared woodlands, is the god who would protect the wild trees discussed in lines 413–53.

511–12 *a life in exile ... in a fatherland*: Virgil echoes his own language in *Eclogue* 1 (see Introduction), but it is not clear whether he has in mind here simple victims of political change or partisans who brought on their own exile by civil violence.

532–4 *the Sabines ... from strength to strength*: the Sabines were Rome's neighbours in the hill region east of Rome: after the trick by which Romulus' men abducted the Sabine women, a retaliatory war ended in alliance and the sharing of the city between Roman and Sabine. Virgil probably speaks of Remus rather than Romulus for metrical reasons (he addresses Romulus in 1.498) rather than as a reminder of Romulus' alleged fratricide. Etruscan power was greatest between the eighth and early fifth centuries: Virgil probably has in mind the Etruscan dynasty of the Tarquins which ruled Rome and brought her new wealth.

536–8 *before a Cretan king ... by splendid Saturn*: the Cretan king is Jupiter, born on Mt. Ida in Crete, and Virgil is returning to the revolutionary moment (described in 1.121) when Jupiter took away from mankind the easy living of his father Saturn's golden age. The last few lines recapitulate the marks of human decline from innocence, in the sacrifice of oxen, men's fellow workers, and development of weapons and warfare.

BOOK THREE

4–7 *who hasn't heard of Eurystheus ... out of ivory*: Juno hated Hercules, her husband's son by the mortal Alcmene, and ensured that he was enslaved to king Eurystheus and had to perform twelve labours. Hercules slew the cruel Egyptian king Busiris who made human sacrifice of strangers. Hylas, Hercules' boy-beloved, was seized by water-nymphs at a pool in Mysia on their journey with the Argonauts (Apollonius' *Argonautica* had recently been translated into Latin by Varro of Atax, but the only Latin treatments of Hylas known to us are later than Virgil's *Georgics*). Delos was the floating island which alone offered Latona a place to give birth to the twins Apollo and Artemis/Diana. Pelops won the hand of the princess Hippodamia ('the horsetamer') of Argos and lordship over the *Pelop*-onnese by cheating her treacherous father Oenomaus in the chariot race. His shoulder was an ivory prosthesis, because the bone had been inadvertently gnawed by a god when the infant Pelops had been served to the gods in a disguised cannibal feast.

9   *live on in the mouths of men*: echo of a famous phrase of the second-
    century epic poet Ennius.

10–11 *the first . . . to bring back to my own place from the heights of Helicon*: like
    Ennius and Lucretius before him, Virgil claims to be first in composing
    this new kind of Latin poetry. The Muses were said to live on Mt.
    Helicon in Boeotia, near Thespiae, which held festivals in their honour in
    Virgil's time.

12 *palms of Idumaea*: the victory prizes in the races are called Idumaean
    because they grew in Palestine.

16 *At its centre I'll place Caesar*: on Virgil's imagined festival to honour
    Octavian, see Introduction pp. xx–xxi).

19 *all Greece will leave the Alpheus . . . Molorchus*: the river Alpheus (cf. line
    180) ran through Olympia, site of the games in honour of Olympian
    Zeus; Molorchus was Hercules' host at Nemea when he founded the
    Nemean Games. Virgil would know of the humble Molorchus from
    Callimachus' poem about this occasion in his *Aitia*.

25–33 *Britons . . . at two far edges of the ocean*: Virgil's list of foreign enemies
    are chiefly those Octavian is expected to defeat (Britain, raided by Julius
    Caesar in 54 and 55, not conquered until 41 CE), India—off the map;
    Egypt (already defeated); Parthia—still to come; the Asian cities which
    had supported Antony but surrendered to Octavian after Antony's defeat,
    and the Niphates range of mountains in Armenia. In ancient geography,
    the Ocean surrounded India as well as Britain, Spain, and North Africa.

35 *scions of Assaracus*: according to Aeneas' genealogy in *Iliad* 20.232–40,
    Assaracus, son of Tros, 'king of the Trojans', was grandfather of Anchises
    and great-grandfather of Aeneas. This was a different branch of the
    family from the false Laomedon, who cheated Apollo over the building of
    Troy's walls (see note to 1.502), who was grandson of Tros by Ilus, and
    himself father of Tithonus (see note to line 48) and Priam.

38–9 *Ixion tied to a rotating wheel . . . the rock that bested everyone*: Ixion
    the Lapith, father of Pirithous, (cf. 2.456 and note) tried to violate
    Hera/Juno, but she turned into a cloud, from which he begat Centaurus,
    the father of the race of Centaurs. Ixion was one of the canonical group of
    sinners punished in Hades. The wheel is traditional, the snakes a novelty
    introduced by Virgil. The rock had to be pushed uphill by another canon-
    ical sinner, Sisyphus of Corinth, but constantly rolled back on him.

43–4 *Cithaeron . . . Epidaurus*: Cithaeron, between Boeotia and Attica, was, like
    Spartan Taygetus, a mountain associated with hunting. Epidaurus on the
    north-east Peloponnese has no known association with horse breeding,
    and scholars have suggested that Virgil wrote 'Epidamnus', in horse-
    breeding Epirus.

48 *first emergence of Tithonus*: the Trojan prince Tithonus, brother of Priam,
    was loved by the dawn goddess who obtained immortality for him but

forgot to request eternal youth. He became a symbol of old age, equivalent of Methuselah.

89 *Cyllarus ... to the rein*: Cyllarus was traditionally ridden by Jupiter's human son Castor, rather than his brother Pollux. The two Dioscuri were worshipped at Rome as patrons of the cavalry. The chariot teams of Mars (Ares) and Achilles are described in *Iliad* 15.119–20 and 16.148–9.

92 *Nimble Saturn, at his wife's arrival*: according to Apollonius' *Argonautica*, Kronos/Saturn was caught by his wife Rhea while wooing the nymph Phillyra, and turned himself into a horse to complete the seduction, producing the centaur Chiron. The rape was on Mt. Pelion in Thessaly, which became Chiron's home.

113–15 *Erichthonius ... The Lapiths*: in *Iliad* 20.219–30, Erichthonius is father of Tros and breeder of three thousand horses; the Hellenistic poet Eratosthenes makes this Trojan prince inventor of the four-horse chariot. The Lapiths are the Thessalian people ruled by Ixion (see note to line 38).

121–2 *Epirus or Mycenae ... Neptune's stable*: again, it is assumed that the best breeds came from Greece—Epirus in the north-west and Peloponnesian Mycenae. On Neptune's creation of the first horse, see note to 1.7–18.

147–53 *there swarms a pest ... Io, daughter of Inachus*: like Varro (2.5.14), Virgil warns against the gadfly (Greek *myops*) that plagues cattle. First he plays on the name of the river Silarus (in Lucania, like Alburnus and the river Tanager) and *asilus*, then glosses it with the learned Greek name *oestrus*. In mythology this gadfly was sent by Hera/Juno to plague her husband's beloved Io. It seems to have been the subject of descriptions in lost poems of Callimachus and Apollonius.

202–4 *the laps of Elis ... Belgian chariots of war*: like the river Alpheus, the small state of Elis stands for Olympia, and the chariot race: the Romans did not use chariots in warfare, but may have modelled their racing chariots on the war-chariots of the Belgae.

219 *the mighty woods of Sila*: again, Virgil is specific; the mountain of Sila was in Bruttium, near the places named in lines 146 ff., but the battle of the bulls (used again as a simile for the battle of human champions in *Aeneid* 12.715) could occur anywhere.

249 *the wilderness of Africa*: Virgil actually names Libya, pointing ahead to the desert landscape of lines 339 ff.

266–81 *the ferocity of mares ... 'mare madness'*: in a number of ancient myths horses behaved as violently as if they were wild beasts. The racing mares of Glaucus, son of Sisyphus, ate their own master, either because he fed them on human flesh or because he denied them access to the stallions. Desire drives them across two wild rivers of Asia Minor, Gargarus and Ascanius, and they are supposed to conceive as they race borne on the violent north and east winds, secreting a fluid in their groin which Virgil calls by its Greek name *hippomanes* (horse-frenzy) and claims is used by witches and poisoners.

291–3 *Parnassian peaks ... Castalia*: these are the heights above Delphi and Apollo's sacred spring.

312 *bucks from Cinyps*: both Cinyps in Libya, and Arcadia (line 314), the hilly region of the Peloponnese associated with Pan, offer sparse pasture only fit for goats.

339–48 *Libyan shepherds ... his enemy surprised*: some of the details of Virgil's nomad (Numidian) shepherds come from ethnographic passages in Sallust's *Jugurtha*, but his comparison of the primitive nomad to the familiar slog of the Roman soldier carrying his pack is original. (It is pure poetic fancy that gives this aboriginal a Cretan quiver and Spartan hound.)

349–51 *Scythia ... back to the central pole*: the geographical limits of 'Scythia' are the Danube and the mountains of Thrace. In the extended description of ultimate winter (lines 352–83), cold and immobility (the penned cattle, the hunted deer buried in snow and frozen on the spot, the natives skulking in underground dugouts) give maximum contrast with the Libyan in constant motion beneath the sun and stars. Virgil's extended account of snow and frozen rivers was copied by Ovid, but his source is not known. See R. F. Thomas, *Lands and Peoples in Roman Poetry: The Ethnographical Tradition* (Cambridge, 1982).

391–2 *that Pan of Arcadia wooed you, / the Moon*: the Virgilian critic Macrobius (*Saturnalia* 5.22.9–10) says that Virgil took from Nicander this myth that Pan disguised himself in a fleece to win the love of the moon goddess (Selene). No source reports any child of this courtship which may have been frustrated.

414–39 *learn to burn juniper ... his three-forked tongue*: Virgil has adapted this section from several passages of Nicander's *Theriaca*, retaining a number of purely Greek names, though he avoids naming the *chersydros* which he describes in detail and sets in south Italian Calabria (lines 425–34).

471 *the onset of these plagues ...*: Virgil moves from preventive measures (sheep dipping) and medicating individual ulcers and sickness to an undated epidemic (line 478) in Noricum (the hinterland of Trieste) of which there is no other record. It leapt across species from cows to dogs to pigs to horses (the detailed symptomology describes the horse, lines 498–514) then back to oxen dying beneath the yoke of the plough: for them Virgil avoids repeating symptoms and substitutes an anthropomorphizing lament over their hard life of toil free of human self-indulgence (lines 515–30). Men scrabble like beasts and the whole order of relationship between creatures disintegrates.

550 *Chiron, son of Phillyra; Melampus, son of Amythaon*: the centaur Chiron (see note to line 92) practised medicine with herbs; Melampus was both doctor and seer. Hence perhaps Virgil's transition from medicine to

religion, invoking the Fury Tisiphone (line 551), normally a punisher of bloodguilt, as symbol of death triumphant.

BOOK FOUR

1 *heaven's gift of honey*: Virgil plunges directly into his theme, stressing both the supernatural aspect of honey, and the resemblance of the hive to a human society, aspects of the bees' nature which he will reiterate through the book (see lines 153–5, 164 ff., and 200–5, for example). He will use epic language and allusions, not to mock the bees, but to stress their delicate vulnerability

15 *Procne, her breast still bearing stains*: the Athenian princess Procne was married to Tereus, king of Thrace, who raped her sister Philomela. In fury, the women murdered Procne's son Itys and fed the child's flesh to his father. When Tereus discovered the crime all three were transformed, he to a hoopoe, Philomela to the nightingale, and Procne to the swallow, which has blood-red breast feathers.

55 *enraptured by such strange delight*: while Virgil stresses the sensitivity of the bees to smell and sound, and their indifference to sexual desire, he credits them with a mysterious emotional life; cf. lines 70 and 149 ff.

68 *two queens*: modern apiarists know that the hive is ruled by a female, but Virgil like most ancients, thought the leader was male and speaks of choosing between two kings or male leaders. The recommendation to kill one 'king' when two are competing (lines 88–91) is found in Varro 3. 16.18, but may be a pointed allusion to Antony as rival of Octavian; Varro also identifies the 'dusty' bees as less healthy (3.16.20).

109–10 *Let there be gardens . . . Priapus of Hellespont*: Italy had imported the cult of the ultra-virile Priapus from Lampsacus on the Hellespont and put home-made wooden herms of the god with his large organ in vegetable gardens to scare away birds and human thieves. Virgil will use the bees' need for flowers as an excuse for his digression (lines 125 ff.) describing the old immigrant gardener's allotment by the river Galaesus in sunny Tarentum.

149–52 *the qualities bestowed on bees by Jupiter . . . that Cretan cave*: when Rhea smuggled the newborn Jupiter to the care of the nymphs in a cave on Mt. Ida in Crete, to hide the baby's cries the Curetes (Rhea's attendants) clashed their cymbals as they danced and the bees, attracted by the noise (cf. line 64 above), fed him with honey.

170–3 *when the Cyclopes . . . Etna groaned beneath the weight of anvils*: the bees' unanimous and unresting devotion to their delicate task is compared by opposites to the diligence of the giant Cyclopes, primitive subhuman creatures like the Nibelungen, who were believed to forge Jupiter's thunderbolts under Mt. Etna in Sicily or the Aeolian islands, because the volcanic smoke suggested the chimney of a forge.

210–11 *Egypt . . . or the Medes*: these nations were seen as willing slaves of their monarchies present or past.

232 *Taÿgete of the Seven Sisters*: the rising of the Pleiades in May.

234 *trying to escape from Pisces*: the setting of the Pleiades in November, although Pisces will only rise later.

246 *a spider, Minerva's fateful enemy*: the Lydian weaver Arachne, whom Minerva turned into a spider out of jealousy at her superior tapestry work.

271 *a flower farmers call 'amellus'*: as with the *asilus*, Virgil gives detailed attention to the powers of this aster-like flower, its name derived from the river Mella in northern Italy.

283–4 *what that great Arcadian keeper/first discovered*: this is Aristaeus, last mentioned (but not named) at 1.14–15 as the patron of woods and keeper of cattle on Ceos. His connection with Arcadia is unknown, but the word translated 'keeper' here not only means master of a herd, but carries the notion of teacher or inventor. Although the character we meet in the narrative seems an immature figure, he emerges as a model of success despite adversity, and success won through piety and dogged attention to instructions—thus the prototype of the good farmer (and good pupil). He will not be named until after the account of Egyptian *bougonia*, at line 317, when we shall meet him in Thessaly. (See Introduction, pp. xxx–xxxi.)

287 *Pellaean people . . . beside Canopus on the Nile*: the ruling people of Egypt were Macedonians (so from Pella), and Canopus just one of the Nile's seven mouths, but the Egyptians are described here as neighbours of the Parthians (called 'archers', line 290, and recalled in the comparison of line 312) and associated with the river itself which comes from the equatorial south—hence 'sun-bronzed Ethiopians' (line 292), in which the adjective translates the Greek name *Aithiopes* ('burnt faces') which was loosely applied to all the known peoples of East Africa. The Romans of this generation knew Egypt from images of the course of the Nile, filled with boats and crocodiles and flanked by villages and temples such as we see on the Nile Mosaic of Palestrina.

317 *Tempe, through which the Peneius flows*: this is the fertile valley of Thessaly, but in lines 363–73, by a kind of magic geography, Virgil makes Cyrene's underwater home the centre of a network of caverns which provide the source of rivers worldwide—from Colchis (the Phasis) and Asia Minor, the Thessalian Enipeus, Roman Tiber and Anio, the Black Sea Hypanis and Caicus (this Mysian river flows into the Aegean through western Turkey), and finally the mysterious Eridanus, sometimes equated with the Po (as it may be here given the reference to 'rich farmlands', line 373), sometimes with other rivers of the west.

320 *directed his complaint to the one who bore him*: Aristaeus may seem childish in this self-pitying lament, but his complaint (lines 321–32) is modelled on that of a hero, Achilles' complaint to his mother in *Iliad* 1.348–56.

Aristaeus is a doubly Homeric figure, taking on the guile and endurance of Menelaus in the second part of his adventure. Virgil has used his protest to recapitulate all the varieties of farming discussed in Books 1–3 (line 327: 'expert care of crops and cattle', lines 329–31: 'fruiting forests ... stalls ... harvest ... vines').

333 *Deep in the river ...*: like the respectable mistress of a Roman house, Aristaeus' mother, the nymph Cyrene, is surrounded by her attendants, preparing the best wool from Miletus (dyed sea-coloured because they are water-nymphs). Their names, chosen for their melodious and foreign sounds, are free invention, though two nymphs are called 'daughters of Oceanus', and one is Arethusa, the nymph of the freshwater spring at Syracuse in Sicily.

345–6 *Clymene, rambling on ... and the joy he stole*: Clymene is telling what may be the oldest tale of adultery (cf. Demodocus' version in *Odyssey* 8): how the sun told Vulcan that his wife Venus was sleeping with Mars and he trapped them in a superfine magic net, but they were unashamed.

347 *all the loves of all the gods, from Chaos' time to ours*: a neat recall of Hesiod's genealogies in *Theogony*.

381 *to Oceanus*: Ocean seems to be worshipped here chiefly as father of the nymphs of woodland and sea whom, as we shall learn at lines 533–4, Aristaeus has offended.

387 *Proteus*: the Old Man of the Sea, Proteus, is gifted with prophecy in *Odyssey* 4.387 ff., but also with the power to change his shape so as to elude capture. Virgil has adapted Aristaeus' adventure from that of Menelaus in Egypt, where Menelaus too is instructed by a nymph, Eidothea. But he has changed location, setting Proteus first in the island of Carpathos, then in Pallene. This is probably an Alexandrian variation since Proteus is also associated with Pallene in a fragment of Callimachus.

392 *even agèd Nereus*: Nereus the sea-god was father of Thetis, and it was Proteus who warned Zeus that he should not mate with Thetis because her son was fated to be mightier than his father. As a result Thetis married the mortal Peleus and became the mother of Achilles.

425–7 *The Dog Star ... half his daily course*: the Dog Star indicates the time of year—high summer—and the sun the time of day—high noon.

433 *like that herdsman in the mountains:* the simile comparing Proteus and his smelly herd of seals to a hill shepherd watching his calves and lambs ties this narrative back to the second part of Book 3.

454 *Orpheus*: this is the first mention of Orpheus or Aristaeus' sexual pursuit of Orpheus' bride, Eurydice, which caused her death by the bite of a water-snake (another link with Book 3). Proteus' tale of Orpheus will extend from here to 527.

460 *her peers, the Dryads:* Eurydice too was a nymph, and so is lamented by the nymphs of Thrace; Cyrene will confirm to her son in lines 534–6 that

he must appease them with sacrifice. Rhodope (line 461) is a Thracian mountain range, Rhesus (line 462) the Thracian king who was treacherously killed by Odysseus and Diomedes (*Iliad* 10) when he came to defend Troy. The Getae (line 463) were a tribe contemporary with Virgil, the Hebrus (cf. line 524) the Thracian river which would carry away Orpheus' severed head, and Orithyia, princess of Athens and sister of Procne and Philomela, was abducted by the north wind to the same cold northern regions.

464–5 *his lyre / a hollowed tortoiseshell*: the Homeric hymn to Hermes tells how Hermes invented the lyre by scooping a tortoise from its shell to make the soundbox of his instrument.

467 *the gorge of Taenarus*: Taenarus, in the region of Sparta, like Avernus in Campania, was believed to be an entrance to Hades.

469–84 *to approach the shades . . . settled to a standstill*: in sixteen lines Virgil includes all the elements of the underworld, taken from *Odyssey* 11 and later sources, which he would develop in the sixth book of the *Aeneid*. He does not even mention that the lord of Hades grants Orpheus' appeal, but describes the souls of the innocent dead enclosed by the rivers Cocytus and Styx, and Tartarus guarded by Cerberus where the sinners (only Ixion is named: cf. note to 3.38–9) are punished by the Furies.

486–7 *Eurydice . . . trailing close behind (as Proserpina/ had decreed)*: only now, and with a painful slowness, does Virgil reveal both the consent and the terms decreed by Proserpina (cf. 1.39) as queen of Hades. This is all the more agonizing as Virgil was the first to claim that Orpheus failed in his quest and lost Eurydice for ever. In Virgil Eurydice speaks now for the first and last time: Orpheus, 'with so much still to say' (line 501), cannot speak, but even after his death his head will repeat her name which will be taken up by the river banks (line 527), as they earlier (line 463) wept at her original death.

502–3 *No longer would the ferryman permit him cross . . . that lay between them*: as Virgil shows in his depiction of Hades at *Aeneid* 6.326–30, Charon only ferried the properly buried dead across Cocytus and the Styx: it was forbidden for him to convey the living (*Aeneid* 6.391). Virgil does not explain how Orpheus had been able to cross into Hades earlier, but Hercules and Theseus had succeeded.

507–22 *For seven whole long months . . . through the land*: Orpheus is now back in Thrace, by the river Strymon, and (line 517) as far north as the river Tanais (the Don, on the north coast of the Black Sea). It is in Thrace that the women in Bacchic frenzy are angered by his lament and tear him apart.

528 *Thus spoke Proteus*: Proteus has told Aristaeus only the cause of his loss; but Cyrene, apparently standing near, moves from past to future, instructing him in the sacrifices he must make.

549 *he did all that his mother bid*: Cyrene too only tells him half of what she knows. When Aristaeus has carried out all the sacrifices and waited patiently, the miracle (line 554) comes as a surprise to him, though Virgil's readers will have been guided to expect something of this kind by the slightly different Egyptian procedure of lines 295–314. With the new swarm of bees the narrative ends; there is no return to Virgil's own apiculture.

558 *Such was the song*: this personal *sphragis*, or 'signing off', contrasts Octavian's military glory at the edges of empire with Virgil himself, his name, the sheltered place of his 'studies of the arts of peace' (line 564) and his works to date. The last line ('you, Tityrus'), echoes the first line of Virgil's first *Eclogue*, but puts the poet himself under the spreading beech tree.

The Oxford World's Classics Website

www.worldsclassics.co.uk

- Browse the full range of Oxford World's Classics online

- Sign up for our monthly e-alert to receive information on new titles

- Read extracts from the Introductions

- Listen to our editors and translators talk about the world's greatest literature with our Oxford World's Classics audio guides

- Join the conversation, follow us on Twitter at OWC_Oxford

- Teachers and lecturers can order inspection copies quickly and simply via our website

www.worldsclassics.co.uk

American Literature

British and Irish Literature

Children's Literature

Classics and Ancient Literature

Colonial Literature

Eastern Literature

European Literature

Gothic Literature

History

Medieval Literature

Oxford English Drama

Poetry

Philosophy

Politics

Religion

The Oxford Shakespeare

A complete list of Oxford World's Classics, including Authors in Context, Oxford English Drama, and the Oxford Shakespeare, is available in the UK from the Marketing Services Department, Oxford University Press, Great Clarendon Street, Oxford OX2 6DP, or visit the website at www.oup.com/uk/worldsclassics.

In the USA, visit www.oup.com/us/owc for a complete title list.

Oxford World's Classics are available from all good bookshops. In case of difficulty, customers in the UK should contact Oxford University Press Bookshop, 116 High Street, Oxford OX1 4BR.

Bhagavad Gita

The Bible Authorized King James Version
  With Apocrypha

Dhammapada

Dharmasūtras

The Koran

The Pañcatantra

**The Sauptikaparvan (from the
  Mahabharata)**

**The Tale of Sinuhe and Other Ancient
  Egyptian Poems**

The Qur'an

Upaniṣads

ANSELM OF CANTERBURY	**The Major Works**
THOMAS AQUINAS	**Selected Philosophical Writings**
AUGUSTINE	**The Confessions**
	On Christian Teaching
BEDE	**The Ecclesiastical History**
HEMACANDRA	**The Lives of the Jain Elders**
KĀLIDĀSA	**The Recognition of Śakuntalā**
MANJHAN	**Madhumalati**
ŚĀNTIDEVA	**The Bodhicaryàvatàra**

A SELECTION OF   **OXFORD WORLD'S CLASSICS**

The Anglo-Saxon World

Beowulf

Lancelot of the Lake

The Paston Letters

Sir Gawain and the Green Knight

Tales of the Elders of Ireland

York Mystery Plays

GEOFFREY CHAUCER   The Canterbury Tales
Troilus and Criseyde

HENRY OF HUNTINGDON   The History of the English People
1000–1154

JOCELIN OF BRAKELOND   Chronicle of the Abbey of Bury
St Edmunds

GUILLAUME DE LORRIS   The Romance of the Rose
and JEAN DE MEUN

WILLIAM LANGLAND   Piers Plowman

SIR THOMAS MALORY   Le Morte Darthur